T0209719

An Analysis of

Hans J. Morgenthau's
Politics Among Nations

Ramon Pacheco Pardo

Published by Macat International Ltd
24:13 Coda Centre, 189 Munster Road, London SW6 6AW.

Distributed exclusively by Routledge
2 Park Square, Milton Park, Abingdon, Oxon OX14 4RN
711 Third Avenue, New York, NY 10017, USA

Routledge is an imprint of the Taylor & Francis Group, an informa business

www.macat.com
info@macat.com

Cataloguing in Publication Data
A catalogue record for this book is available from the British Library.
Library of Congress Cataloguing-in-Publication Data is available upon request.
Cover illustration: Etienne Gilfillan

ISBN 978-1-912303-40-3 (hardback)
ISBN 978-1-912127-17-7 (paperback)
ISBN 978-1-912282-28-9 (e-book)

Notice
The information in this book is designed to orientate readers of the work under analysis,
to elucidate and contextualise its key ideas and themes, and to aid in the development
of critical thinking skills. It is not meant to be used, nor should it be used, as a
substitute for original thinking or in place of original writing or research. References and
notes are provided for informational purposes and their presence does not constitute
endorsement of the information or opinions therein. This book is presented solely for
educational purposes. It is sold on the understanding that the publisher is not engaged
to provide any scholarly advice. The publisher has made every effort to ensure that
this book is accurate and up-to-date, but makes no warranties or representations with
regard to the completeness or reliability of the information it contains. The information
and the opinions provided herein are not guaranteed or warranted to produce particular
results and may not be suitable for students of every ability. The publisher shall not be
liable for any loss, damage or disruption arising from any errors or omissions, or from
the use of this book, including, but not limited to, special, incidental, consequential or
other damages caused, or alleged to have been caused, directly or indirectly, by the
information contained within.

CONTENTS

THE MACAT LIBRARY

The Macat Library is a series of unique academic explorations of seminal works in the humanities and social sciences – books and papers that have had a significant and widely recognised impact on their disciplines. It has been created to serve as much more than just a summary of what lies between the covers of a great book. It illuminates and explores the influences on, ideas of, and impact of that book. Our goal is to offer a learning resource that encourages critical thinking and fosters a better, deeper understanding of important ideas.

Each publication is divided into three Sections: Influences, Ideas, and Impact. Each Section has four Modules. These explore every important facet of the work, and the responses to it.

This Section-Module structure makes a Macat Library book easy to use, but it has another important feature. Because each Macat book is written to the same format, it is possible (and encouraged!) to cross-reference multiple Macat books along the same lines of inquiry or research. This allows the reader to open up interesting interdisciplinary pathways.

To further aid your reading, lists of glossary terms and people mentioned are included at the end of this book (these are indicated by an asterisk [*] throughout) – as well as a list of works cited.

Macat has worked with the University of Cambridge to identify the elements of critical thinking and understand the ways in which six different skills combine to enable effective thinking.
Three allow us to fully understand a problem; three more give us the tools to solve it. Together, these six skills make up the **PACIER** model of critical thinking. They are:

ANALYSIS – understanding how an argument is built
EVALUATION – exploring the strengths and weaknesses of an argument
INTERPRETATION – understanding issues of meaning

CREATIVE THINKING – coming up with new ideas and fresh connections
PROBLEM-SOLVING – producing strong solutions
REASONING – creating strong arguments

To find out more, visit **WWW.MACAT.COM.**

CRITICAL THINKING AND *POLITICS AMONG NATIONS*

Primary critical thinking skill: REASONING
Secondary critical thinking skill: EVALUATION

Hans Morgenthau's *Politics Among Nations* is a classic of political science, built on the firm foundation of Morgenthau's watertight reasoning skills.

The central aim of reasoning is to construct a logical and persuasive argument that carefully organizes and supports its conclusions – often around a central concept or scheme of argumentation. Morgenthau's subject was international relations – the way in which the world's nations interact, and come into conflict or peace – a topic which was of vital importance during the unstable wake of the Second World War. To the complex problem of understanding the ways in which the post-war nations were jostling for power, Morgenthau brought a comprehensive schema: the concept of "realism" – or, in other words, the idea that every nation will act so as to maximise its own interests. From this basis, Morgenthau builds a systematic argument for a pragmatic approach to international relations in which nations seeking consensus should aim for a balance of power, grounding relations between states in understandings of how the interests of individual nations can be maximized.

Though seismic shifts in international politics after the Cold War undeniably altered the landscape of international relations, Morgenthau's dispassionate reasoning about the nature of our world remains influential to this day.

ABOUT THE AUTHOR OF THE ORIGINAL WORK

Hans J. Morgenthau was born in Germany in 1904. He emigrated in the 1930s as Hitler's National Socialist party began to make life more difficult for German Jews. His travels took him through Spain, as the fascists were fighting the Civil War they would eventually win, and finally to the United States in 1937. Having seen nationalist ideas destroy great nations and millions of people, Morgenthau came to believe strongly in the political importance of maintaining a balance of power between nations. He died in New York in 1980 at the age of 76.

ABOUT THE AUTHOR OF THE ANALYSIS

Dr. Ramon Pacheco Pardo is Senior Lecturer in International Relations at King's College London. He holds a PhD in International Relations form the London School of Economics and is a research associate at the Lau China Institute and the Global Studies Institute in Hong Kong. Dr Pacheco Pardo has held visiting positions at the Lee Kuan Yew School of Public Policy and Korea University, and sits on the editorial board of *Global Studies Journal*.

ABOUT MACAT

GREAT WORKS FOR CRITICAL THINKING

Macat is focused on making the ideas of the world's great thinkers accessible and comprehensible to everybody, everywhere, in ways that promote the development of enhanced critical thinking skills.

It works with leading academics from the world's top universities to produce new analyses that focus on the ideas and the impact of the most influential works ever written across a wide variety of academic disciplines. Each of the works that sit at the heart of its growing library is an enduring example of great thinking. But by setting them in context – and looking at the influences that shaped their authors, as well as the responses they provoked – Macat encourages readers to look at these classics and game-changers with fresh eyes. Readers learn to think, engage and challenge their ideas, rather than simply accepting them.

'Macat offers an amazing first-of-its-kind tool for
interdisciplinary learning and research. Its focus on works
that transformed their disciplines and its rigorous approach,
drawing on the world's leading experts and educational institutions,
opens up a world-class education to anyone.'

Andreas Schleicher
Director for Education and Skills, Organisation for Economic
Co-operation and Development

'Macat is taking on some of the major challenges in university
education … They have drawn together a strong team of active
academics who are producing teaching materials that are
novel in the breadth of their approach.'

Prof Lord Broers,
former Vice-Chancellor of the University of Cambridge

'The Macat vision is exceptionally exciting. It focuses
upon new modes of learning which analyse and explain seminal texts
which have profoundly influenced world thinking and so social and
economic development. It promotes the kind of critical thinking
which is essential for any society and economy.
This is the learning of the future.'

Rt Hon Charles Clarke, former UK Secretary of State for Education

'The Macat analyses provide immediate access to the critical
conversation surrounding the books that have shaped their
respective discipline, which will make them an invaluable resource
to all of those, students and teachers, working in the field.'

Professor William Tronzo, University of California at San Diego

WAYS IN TO THE TEXT

KEY POINTS

- German-born Hans J. Morgenthau (1904–80) is one of the most important scholars in the history of international relations*—the branch of political science that studies the interactions between states, with a particular focus on foreign policies.

- *Politics Among Nations* lays out the tenets of realism*—a theoretical approach to international relations founded on the idea that a state's behavior is driven by the desire to accumulate more power than other states.

- Realism remains one of the key theoretical approaches to the study of international relations today.

Who Was Hans J. Morgenthau?

Published in 1948, *Politics Among Nations: The Struggle for Power and Peace* confirmed Hans J. Morgenthau as a key figure in the history of international relations. The work's key argument is that relations between nations are defined by a desire to accumulate the greatest amount of power. This is the foundation of the theory of international relations known as realism.

Morgenthau was born in Germany in 1904; he left during the 1930s as, being Jewish, the rise of Nazism* made it impossible for him to work in academia there. Traveling first to Switzerland and then to Spain, he finally emigrated to the United States in 1937. Between 1943 and 1973, Morgenthau was a professor at the University of Chicago, where he wrote and published *Politics Among Nations*. He later moved to the City University of New York. After the publication of *Politics Among Nations*, Morgenthau continued to defend his realist view of international relations; in the years of tension between the United States and the Soviet Union*—the Cold War,* which began in 1947—most of his work focused on American foreign policy. He was an active advisor to several US administrations until his death in 1980 at the age of 76.[1]

A student of law and philosophy,[2] Morgenthau also wrote on international law and morality. He based his approach to political science on the notion that law and morality serve to limit the actions states might take when seeking to accumulate power. Although this idea seems to belong more to liberalism,* a political philosophy founded on notions of liberty and equality, Morgenthau is nonetheless considered to be one of the founders, if not the key figure, of realist thought.

What Does *Politics Among Nations* Say?

Politics Among Nations puts forward a realist theory of international relations, based on the idea that all states have the accumulation of power as their main goal. Dominance, realist thinkers believe, guarantees security in an anarchical* international system (that is, an international system with no central authority whatsoever). States do not want to obtain the sort of gains that might also benefit another state; they seek "relative gains,"* which can be measured directly in comparison to another state. Relative power guarantees that a state will maintain its dominant position over other states, and therefore will be secure.

Politics Among Nations first lays out Morgenthau's realist theory—

what he calls the "Six Principles of Political Realism."[3] These principles are then developed in parts two through four, which are a very sophisticated analysis of the concept of power in international relations.[4] In parts five and six, Morgenthau discusses the two main checks and balances in the search for power—international morality and international law.[5] In part seven he tests his theory with the case of the post-World War II* international system.[6] Finally, in parts eight through ten, he discusses the issue of peace.[7]

Morgenthau's main argument is that if a state's goal is simply to have more power than another state, then it is possible for there to be a balance of power.* In this situation no one state has (or even wants) *all* the power. This then brings stability to the international system, because states are less likely to attack each other when the level of their power—or that of the group of states they belong to—is similar to their opponent's. In opposition to Morgenthau's theory is that of liberal idealism,* which takes the approach that stability and security are based on reaching a negotiated solution when there is conflict between two or more actors. This is known as accommodation.* According to Morgenthau, liberal idealism is flawed because it cannot account for countries that seek to accumulate power at the expense of others.

In the six decades and more since *Politics Among Nations* was first published, its ideas have fallen in and out of fashion. Morgenthau wrote the work at the outset of the Cold War, when the world's fate seemed to hinge on the contest between two nuclear-armed superpowers:* the United States and the Soviet Union. The Cold War's abrupt end caught everyone in the field of international relations by surprise. The balance of power, held between two poles for more than a generation, had shifted seemingly overnight. As more states staked their claim to power on the world's stage, critics and thought leaders in the field of international relations pinned their theories on a variety of other frameworks, including:

- Neorealism*—a theory claiming there is no central authority acting over sovereign* states and that states, being self-interested, do not care about the interests of other states
- Neoliberalism*—a theory claiming states are, or should be, concerned with *absolute gains** (increase in powers that might benefit both it and another state) rather than *relative gains* to other states (increases in power that only benefit a single state)
- Neoclassical realism*—a theory claiming state actions can be explained both by *differences in systems*—the balance of power, for example—and by *differences in thinking*—what each state thinks the intentions of other states are, for example, or policies the political elite are lobbying for.

The US invasions of Afghanistan* and Iraq* in the early twenty-first century returned Morgenthau's ideas to the forefront once more. *Politics Among Nations* is currently in its seventh edition.

Why Does *Politics Among Nations* Matter?

Published in the aftermath of World War II and during the early stages of the Cold War, *Politics Among Nations* became a very important text. It shaped thinking in the field of international relations for decades, pitting the idea of realism against the notion of liberal idealism. Today, political scientists deal with a multiplicity of "isms"—but Morgenthau's work helped define the field.

If the purpose of research in the field of international relations is to predict future behavior of states, then some critics find that Morgenthau's work falls short. They have contended that his realist theory is not rigorous enough, making it impossible to use as a predictive tool. But if the purpose of international relations studies is to understand the workings of states and their leaders then *Politics Among Nations* offers a rich source of ideas. Since his ideas came back into prominence in the 1990s, scholars have worked on Morgenthau's text to develop a better understanding of his ideas. Realist scholars in particular base their understanding of the international system on the ideas laid out in *Politics Among Nations.*

Morgenthau and his ideas influenced US foreign policy in the early years of the Cold War. After *Politics Among Nations* was published in 1948 Morgenthau joined the US Department of State's Planning Committee sessions.[8] He supported a policy of active containment* to deal with the threat that the Soviet Union would seek to spread communism.* In order to combat this threat, the United States intended to mount a clear show of military strength against the Soviet Union, while working behind the scenes to stop the spread of the ideology they saw as directly opposed to democracy.* Containment remained America's foreign policy throughout the 1950s. Adherents of liberalism supported the more diplomatic policy of "accommodation" (that is, finding resolutions through negotiation).

Whether or not it has had a lasting effect on foreign policy, *Politics Among Nations* helped to change the way scholars develop international relations theories. In the decades before its publication, international relations scholars did not base their work on scientific method,* but on discussion of their ideas. Morgenthau's book helped to popularize the use of the scientific method to make and justify an argument, despite the criticism that he was not sufficiently rigorous himself. Important books subsequently followed a more scientific approach; among them were influential works such as Kenneth Waltz's* *Theory of International Politics* (1979), Robert O. Keohane's* *After Hegemony: Cooperation and Discord in the World Economy* (1984), and Alexander Wendt's* *Social Theory of International Politics* (1999).

Morgenthau introduced realism as a theory. But he also introduced the scientific method as the way to study international relations.

NOTES

1   Christoph Frei, *Hans J. Morgenthau: An Intellectual Biography* (Baton Rouge, LA: Louisiana State University Press, 2001), 29–31.

2   Frei, *Morgenthau* , 208–26.

3   Hans J. Morgenthau, *Politics Among Nations: The Struggle for Power and Peace*, 7th ed. (New York: McGraw-Hill, 2006), 3–16.

4   Morgenthau, *Politics Among Nations*, 27–231.

5   Morgenthau, *Politics Among Nations*, 235–334.

6   Morgenthau, *Politics Among Nations*, 337–97.

7   Morgenthau, *Politics Among Nations*, 401–568.

8   Frei, *Morgenthau*, 77.

SECTION 1
INFLUENCES

MODULE 1
THE AUTHOR AND THE HISTORICAL CONTEXT

KEY POINTS

- *Politics Among Nations* can be considered the founding text of realism,* one of the most important theories of international relations.*

- Morgenthau suffered from the rising anti-Semitism* in his home country, Germany, and witnessed preparations for World War II,* which affected his writings.

- *Politics Among Nations* applied the lessons of the first two world wars to the emerging Cold War.*

Why Read This Text?

Published in 1948, just three years after the end of World War II, Hans J. Morgenthau's *Politics Among Nations: The Struggle for Power and Peace* is one of the twentieth century's most important books in the field of international relations. In it, Morgenthau lays out his theory about how states interact with each other, based on timeless insights about human behavior under anarchy* (a system defined by a lack of any kind of governing authority).

Morgenthau believes international politics is really just an extension of human behavior into relations between states. Humans have a will to gain power—the ability to coerce and to dominate others. Morgenthau does not see "states" and "statesmen" as particularly distinct from one another. Statesmen control states, and they are human, prone to human failings and weaknesses. Unlike many other realists, Morgenthau considered this situation to be a "tragedy."[1] He

> ❝ Hans Morgenthau … has been dubbed 'the Pope' of international relations. He is certainly the best known, even though he often claimed to be the least understood, of the classical, realist thinkers in the twentieth century. ❞
>
> Martin Griffiths, *Fifty Key Thinkers in International Relations*

called for a balance between morality and the "national interest" (something he defined as gaining and maintaining power).

Although *Politics Among Nations* is famous as an analysis of power, Morgenthau saw it as a guide on the limitations of power, and the importance of ideas in international politics. Perhaps his most timeless criticism, as a speaker of "truth to power," was that no nation should confuse its national interest with a moral crusade—to do so results in unnecessary suffering, and the eventual failure of that nation. One of the most influential works in the study of international politics, *Politics Among Nations* is still at the heart of many new debates in the field.

Author's Life

Hans J. Morgenthau was born in Coburg, Germany in 1904, to a middle-class Jewish family. Following the end of World War I* in 1918, German anti-Semitism—hostility towards Jewish people—became deadly. Growing up amid this growing danger shaped Morgenthau's entire life. "My relationship to the social environment," Morgenthau wrote in 1922, "is determined by three facts: I am a German, I am a Jew, and I have matured in the period following the war." Morgenthau considered this political and social environment "destructive of the ties of love and friendship or brutal insults, as a crying injustice and a dishonoring humiliation."[2] Power politics*—politics conducted by threats and aggression—affected him, personally, at home in Germany, and led to war twice in his lifetime.

By 1935 he was teaching in Madrid, where he witnessed the early stages of the Spanish Civil War* between the fascists* and the democrats. With hostility towards Jews growing in Germany, and Spain already at war, Morgenthau emigrated to the United States in 1937. He joined the University of Chicago faculty in 1943.[3]

Morgenthau stayed in Chicago for 30 years, writing *Politics Among Nations* while on the Chicago faculty. Throughout his career, he participated in debates concerning foreign policy and advised several US administrations on foreign policy. Most notably, in the 1950s and 1960s he opposed America's involvement in the Vietnam War.* In 1973 he moved to the City University of New York. He died in 1980.[4]

Author's Background

Morgenthau wrote *Politics Among Nations* in the immediate aftermath of World War II. Although he had emigrated to America two years before the war officially began in Europe, he had witnessed first hand the turbulence leading up to the war. In 1939, Nazi* Germany invaded Poland, and conflict broke out across Europe and then around the world. In the ensuing years, Britain, France, the Soviet Union,* and the United States (together known as the Allied Powers) responded to the threat posed by Germany, Japan, and Italy (known as the Axis Powers).

In 1945, the Allies claimed victory against both Germany and Japan—but the conflict had claimed some 75 million lives, including as many as 17 million civilians murdered as a result of the Nazi government's genocidal policies toward Jews, homosexuals, and ethnic minorities.

Politics Among Nations was not just shaped by the war that preceded it; it was also shaped by the hostility that would follow—the Cold War, which lasted from roughly 1947 to 1991. The Cold War was not a well-defined conflict, but was instead a period of tension between the two global superpowers* that had emerged after World War II—the United States and the Soviet Union. Although both states possessed nuclear weapons, it was understood that using them would produce "mutually assured destruction." So the Cold War combatants did not engage in open warfare. Instead they relied on proxy wars* (sponsoring opposing sides in military conflicts), diplomatic intrigue, and various global alliances.

In the early stages of the Cold War, there was much debate about how the US and its allies, together known as "the Western bloc,"* should respond to the perceived threat of the Soviet Union.[5] George Kennan,* an American diplomat and a prominent realist* thinker (that is, he shared Morgenthau's belief that states were motivated by self-interest to seek power), was an advisor in the US embassy in Moscow. Kennan turned out to be "X," the anonymous author of an article published in *Foreign Affairs* in 1946, at the outset of the Cold War. "The political personality of Soviet power as we know it today," Kennan wrote, "is the product of ideology and circumstances." The ideology Kennan referred to was that of the Soviet president Joseph Stalin* and the inner circle of advisors he inherited from the revolutionary leaders who had created the Soviet Union; the "circumstances" he meant were "the power which they now have exercised for nearly three decades in Russia."[6] The United States, in other words, saw a new kind of threat emerging in the East. Morgenthau's work would address this.

NOTES

1   Hans J. Morgenthau, *Scientific Man Versus Power Politics* (Chicago: University of Chicago Press, 1974), 203.

2   Hans Morgenthau, "Fragment of an Intellectual Biography," in *Truth and Tragedy: A Tribute to Hans. J Morgenthau*, eds. Kenneth W. Thompson and Robert J. Myers (New Brunswick: Transaction Publishers, 1984), 1–2.

3   Christoph Frei, *Hans J. Morgenthau: An Intellectual Biography* (Baton Rouge, LA: Louisiana State University Press, 2001), 70–1.

4   Frei, *Morgenthau*, 208–26.

5   Thomas J. McCormick, *America's Half-Century: United States Foreign Policy in the Cold War and After* (Baltimore: John Hopkins University Press, 1995), 93–5.

6   X (George F. Kennan), "The Sources of Soviet Conduct," *Foreign Affairs* 65, no. 4 (1987): 852.

ACADEMIC CONTEXT

KEY POINTS

- The study of international relations* is, at its core, an analysis of power and its limitations.

- The argument that the more powerful will dominate the less powerful when there is no recourse to law is very old; it was proposed in ancient Greece.

- Morgenthau was deeply influenced by the work of historical authors, claiming that human nature is eternally flawed since we are naturally hungry for power.

The Work in its Context

Hans J. Morgenthau's *Politics Among Nations: The Struggle for Power and Peace* shaped the field of international relations for the second half of the twentieth century. When it was published in 1948, international relations was still a relatively new academic field. The University of Aberystwyth in Wales had established the first department of international relations (then called international politics) in 1919. While academics and others had long studied domestic politics, different factors come into play when power and politics cross borders. In any given country, politics operates in well-defined power structures. When two people have a dispute, they can appeal to authority, such as a judge or police force, in their disputes with one another. But in the international system there are no judges or police forces, and countries look after their own interests. The result is anarchy.*

As long as we have gathered together in political association, groups have had to relate to one another. Unsurprisingly, then, the

> ❝ Morgenthau was the most theoretical and academically influential of the school [realism] ... His gifts as a teacher, lecturer, and writer made him a person of great influence who challenged the conventional wisdom at a time when the United States was trying to come to grips with its new role in the world in the wake of the World War II. ❞
>
> Sanford Lakoff, *Ten Political Ideas that Have Shaped the Modern World*

analysis of political relationships under anarchy has a very long history indeed. But what makes Morgenthau's inquiry distinctive is its focus on power: What is power? How do individuals (whether cities, individuals, or states) use it? How will those individuals interact when they have only themselves to rely on?

Overview of the Field

The ancient Greek historian Thucydides* may have been the first to lay out the principles of pure power politics*—the politics of threat and aggression, a cornerstone of realism.* In his *History of the Peloponnesian War* Thucydides dramatizes a dialogue between the envoys of powerful Athens and the tiny island of Melos. The "Melian Dialogue" encapsulates the logic of power politics perfectly. "In terms of practicality," writes Thucydides, "the dominant exact what they can and the weak concede what they must."[1] In other words, when it comes to states fighting with armies, there is no appeal to "justice." There is only the contest of strength.

Some two thousand years later, the Italian political historian Niccolò Machiavelli'* made a practical application of Thucydides' observation. In his 1513 work *The Prince*, Machiavelli said he aimed to uncover the "effectual truth of the matter [of politics] rather than its imagined one."[2] Machiavelli based his theory of "effectual truth"—what actually works in politics—on the observation that humans are "ungrateful, fickle, simulators and deceivers, avoiders of danger, and greedy for gain … a wretched lot," who will always betray when they can, and therefore must be controlled through force.[3] This leads to his famous conclusion that, when one aims for political control, "it is much safer" for a prince "to be feared than to be loved."[4] The national interest—often called a *raison d'état**—is to be powerful, and preserve itself against outside threats at all cost.

In 1651, the English philosopher Thomas Hobbes's* book *Leviathan* took this philosophy one step further. Hobbes wrote that before entering into societies of laws (states), humans lived in a "state of nature" with no rules or authority. Human nature, as Hobbes sees it, is greedy and violent. Unless constrained by authority, a hungry man will slay another to get his food, and a man with food will see all other men as possible threats and kill them preemptively.[5] This is the key concept of anarchy—in a lawless realm, the only rules are those of power, and the powerful will take what they please.

Academic Influences

Politics Among Nations continues the tradition of these thinkers but adds an element of reflection to their brute realism. Like Thucydides, Machiavelli, and Hobbes, Morgenthau recognizes that "international politics is of necessity power politics."[6] However, he also includes a moral dimension. He sees the tragedy power politics can create. He stated this clearly in *Scientific Man Versus Power Politics*, a book he published two years before *Politics Among Nations*, where he noted "the tragic presence of evil in all political action."[7]

Politics Among Nations is rife with classical references—to Thucydides, Machiavelli, Hobbes, and dozens more thinkers and political figures. Morgenthau grounded his theory in a proud tradition of thinking about the ugly realities of politics. He quotes Thucydides:

"of men we believe that it is a necessary law of their nature that they rule wherever they can."[8]

Morgenthau's book draws on the ideas of many thinkers. But his achievement was to put these ideas together with conversations he was having with his contemporaries, and organize them into a new, more systematic world view. Unlike Thucydides, who embedded his political theory in the midst of his account of a war between Athens and Sparta, Morgenthau does not ground his analysis in the "particulars" of politics. Instead, he attempts to look beyond historical facts to determine the fundamental "forces that determine politics among nations."[9]

NOTES

1   Thucydides, *The Peloponnesian War*, trans. Martin Hammond (Oxford: Oxford University Press, 2009), 302.

2   Niccolò Machiavelli, *The Prince*, trans. Peter Bondanella (Oxford: Oxford World's Classics, 2005), 53.

3   Machiavelli, *The Prince*, 58.

4   Machiavelli, *The Prince*, 58.

5   Thomas Hobbes, *Leviathan*, ed. J. C. A. Gaskin (Oxford: Oxford University Press, 1998), 85.

6   Hans J. Morgenthau, *Politics Among Nations: The Struggle for Power and Peace*, 7th ed. (New York: McGraw-Hill, 2006), 35.

7   Hans J. Morgenthau, *Scientific Man Versus Power Politics* (Chicago: University of Chicago Press, 1974), 203.

8   Thucydides, quoted in Hans J. Morgenthau, *Politics Among Nations*, 38.

9   Morgenthau, *Politics Among Nations*, 22.

MODULE 3
THE PROBLEM

KEY POINTS

- *Politics Among Nations* asks why conflict defines international affairs, and how considerations of power and utopia* (a "perfect," perhaps unrealizable state of affairs) can be balanced.

- *Politics Among Nations* was part of a debate between the schools of idealism* (according to which, among other things, problems between nations can be resolved by negotiation) and realism* (according to which nations are interested, first and foremost, in power). In the book's wake, realism became the standard way of viewing international relations.*

- Morgenthau made the realism of the early twentieth century more systematic, allowing it to claim its place as a distinctive theory in its own right.

Core Question

Hans J. Morgenthau's *Politics Among Nations: The Struggle for Power and Peace* was not the first work to apply realism to the field of international relations. The British historian E. H. Carr* wrote in *The Twenty Years' Crisis* (his work on the period between the two World Wars): "Every political situation contains … elements of utopia and reality, of morality and power."[1]

In the twentieth century, scholars debated the extent to which each drive—to make the world a better place, or to dominate the world as it is—defined international politics. During the first half of the twentieth century, the core question of international relations was:

> ❝ It will be our wish and purpose that the processes of peace, when they are begun, shall be absolutely open and that they shall involve and permit henceforth no secret understandings of any kind. The day of conquest and aggrandizement is gone by; so is also the day of secret covenants entered into in the interest of particular governments and likely at some unlooked-for moment to upset the peace of the world. ❞
>
> Woodrow Wilson, "Fourteen Points"

What makes states behave the way they do and can this behavior change? This is the very question Hans Morgenthau sought to address in *Politics Among Nations*.

Scholars of international relations have approached this question in a number of different ways. In fact, as one scholar puts it, we might think of international relations as a series of "great debates" of which the first was "between the 'idealists' … and 'realists' in the 1930s and 1940s," who sought to understand the failure of Europe's "balance of power"* culminating in World War I.*[2]

The debate between idealism and realism continues. On the one hand, there are those who believe that cooperation defines relations among states; others argue that states have to maximize their power to fend for themselves. These two conceptions of relations among states inform the modern versions of idealism and realism—neoliberalism* and neorealism.*

The Participants

With *Politics Among Nations*, Morgenthau joined an ongoing discussion about how to make the international system stable and peaceful—by making laws (the idealist position) or by balancing power (the realist position).

The British journalist and politician Norman Angell,* one of the most prominent idealists of the early twentieth century, had, in 1909, outlined the major features of idealist thought: state economies are so interdependent* and so entwined with trade and industry that countries no longer have anything to gain from fighting one another.[3] His contemporary, the English geographer Halford Mackinder* and a sort of "pre-realist" thinker, meanwhile argued that "the balance of political power" depends on which state controls the Eurasian "heartland."[4] World War I shattered both these positions. The war illustrated that the power and interests of nations drive state action—not trade dynamics or geography.

As World War I wound down, US president Woodrow Wilson,* a former academic with a doctorate in political science, outlined a theory of cooperation among states: a position that came to be known as liberal idealism. In his famous "Fourteen Points" speech of 1918, he called for a peace of reconciliation after the war. Among the most important points he made in the speech was his plea that "a general association of nations must be formed … affording mutual guarantees of political independence and territorial integrity … guaranteed by international covenant."[5] Wilson believed that even though states may live in anarchy,* they could make rules all would follow and associate with one another in good faith.

The American theologian and ethicist Reinhold Niebuhr,* however, disagreed. "As individuals," Niebuhr wrote in 1932 in his *Moral Man and Immoral Society*, "men believe they ought to love and serve each other … [as] racial, economic, and national groups they take for themselves, whatever their power can command."[6] Niebuhr saw the Wilsonian* faith in international rules and order as a kind of dangerous tragedy. In trusting humanity to be good, the idealists run the risk of allowing them to act their worst.

The Contemporary Debate

Morgenthau dove directly into this debate with *Politics Among Nations*. He saw idealism as dangerously naïve, and felt realism needed to be more systematic. Niebuhr, a fellow realist, was one of Morgenthau's most important influences. They admired each other greatly—in their letters, each claimed the other as his primary source of inspiration.[7] Morgenthau and Niebuhr shared a conception of humans as predisposed to bad actions. Left unchecked, men would act selfishly, disregard the needs of others, betray promises, and use force. "The most significant difference [between Morgenthau and Niebuhr] is in the area of the relationship of ethics to politics."[8]

In essence, Morgenthau believed in a concept called the "autonomy of politics," meaning that "the state has no right" to allow moral commitments to get in the way of its one and only task—protecting its citizens.[9] However, Morgenthau did not endorse this. He merely acknowledged it as a somewhat tragic truth.

Niebuhr believed that our flawed nature as humans means we cannot achieve perfect morality—especially amid the anarchy (that is, the lawlessness) that characterizes international affairs. However, he felt that states' "self-regard and power impulse" does not need to override "loyalty to values, cultures, and civilizations of wider and higher scope than the interests of the nations."[10] Niebuhr did not publish any work touching on international relations until after Morgenthau wrote *Politics Among Nations*. But the two had no doubt exchanged views in private before Niebuhr weighed in on the subject.

NOTES

1   E. H. Carr, *The Twenty Years' Crisis, 1919–1939: An Introduction to the Study of International Relations* (New York: Harper and Row, 1964), 119.

2   Brian Schmidt, introduction to *International Relations and the First Great Debate*, ed. Brian Schmidt (London: Routledge, 2012), 4.

3   Norman Angell, *The Great Illusion: A Study of the Relation of Military Power to National Advantage* (Project Gutenberg: Ebook, 2012), 186.

4   Halford Mackinder, "The Geographical Pivot of History," *The Geographical Journal* 23, no. 4 (1904): 437.

5   Woodrow Wilson, "President Wilson's Message to Congress, January 8, 1918," accessed April 8, 2015, http://www.ourdocuments.gov/doc.php?flash=true&doc=62.

6   Reinhold Niebuhr, *Moral Man and Immoral Society* (New York: Charles Scribner's Sons, 1932), 9.

7   William E. Scheuerman, *Morgenthau* (Cambridge: Polity Press, 2009), 56–7.

8   Ronald Stone, *Prophetic Realism: Beyond Militarism and Pacifism in an Age of Terror* (New York: T&T Clark International, 2005), 40.

9   Hans J. Morgenthau, *Politics Among Nations: The Struggle for Power and Peace*, 7th ed. (New York: McGraw-Hill, 2006), 12–13.

10 Reinhold Niebuhr, *Man's Nature and His Communities: Essays on the Dynamics and Enigmas of Man's Personal and Social Existence* (New York: Charles Scribner's Sons, 1965), 76–7.

MODULE 4
THE AUTHOR'S CONTRIBUTION

KEY POINTS

- Morgenthau aimed to create a theory of international politics that would allow students and statesmen to understand the fundamental forces that define political action.

- Morgenthau's approach involved observing real historical facts, avoiding scientific oversimplification.

- The originality of *Politics Among Nations* was not its realist* perspective (roughly, its assumptions that international relations* were defined by the pursuit of power), but rather its attempt to make a "forward looking" theory that went beyond mere description.

Author's Aims

In *Politics Among Nations: The Struggle for Power and Peace,* Hans J. Morgenthau aimed "to present a theory of international politics" that would "bring order and meaning to a mass of phenomena that without it would remain disconnected and unintelligible."[1] Moreover, this theory should be tested empirically* (that is, with deduction based on observable evidence) and should not rely on abstract and untested formulations about international relations. In other words, Morgenthau not only wanted to create a theory, he also wanted to test it to ensure that it objectively described and anticipated behavior in international politics. This approach set *Politics Among Nations* apart from previous works on international relations that made assertions about international politics without testing them.

Morgenthau also wanted to set up the case against liberal idealism* and its assumptions that, for example, tension between nations could

> ❝ This book purports to present a theory of international politics. The test by which such a theory must be judged is not a priori and abstract but empirical and pragmatic. ❞
>
> Hans J. Morgenthau, *Politics Among Nations*

be resolved through dialogue alone; he saw this understanding of "the struggle for power from the international scene" as dangerously naïve.[2] Morgenthau believed that "it would be useless and even self destructive" to cure any group of the desire for power "while leaving it extant in others," because "those who might be cured would simply fall victims to the power of others."[3]

As Morgenthau sees it, power struggles are natural to humanity and affect all relationships. From the family unit to dealings between states, every relationship can be seen through the lens of power—or lack of it. The only difference between domestic and international politics is that the state constrains its citizens' actions with strong laws. But in the international sphere, states have no such constraints. In Morgenthau's view, the only way states would ever sacrifice this desire for power would be if they were forced to do so. To believe otherwise, he felt, is not only wrong—it's dangerous.

Approach

Morgenthau had a complicated approach to international politics. While more systematic than his predecessors, he also remained very cautious about making too many claims about politics as a science. Science is replicable. The same action will always have the same result: an apple dropped from a tree a dozen times will always smash the same way. But politics is different; one country invading another may have a range of different results and repercussions. And so, for Morgenthau, politics could not be a science.

Although Morgenthau believed that the events political analysts "must try to understand are, on the one hand, unique,"[4] he did acknowledge that in some ways political events can be very consistent, being "manifestations of social forces" which are "the product of human nature in action."[5] And human nature tends to be consistent.

So are political matters too complex to understand? Or are they simple enough to predict? In *Politics Among Nations*, Morgenthau tries to locate the truth somewhere between these two extremes. He argues that "knowledge of the forces that determine politics among nations" is linked to knowledge about the forces that are located in human nature.[6] Therefore, an understanding of human nature serves to help us understand the ways in which states behave towards each other.

Contribution in Context

Morgenthau based *Politics Among Nations* on an understanding of power politics*—that is, the kind of politics enacted through threat and aggression—which has very ancient roots. Notions such as the inevitability of conflict and its origins in human nature were discussed in ancient Greece, for example.

But even so, Morgenthau's approach was original in many ways. While previous theories simply described past events, his was genuinely forward looking. With a distinctive understanding of power rooted in "biopsychology,"* the natural drives and desires of human beings, he derived his theory of politics from universal principles such as "the drives to live, to propagate, and to dominate [that] are common to all men."[7]

Morgenthau entered into a conversation with thinkers such as the British scholar E. H. Carr,* who saw realism* as a kind of critique of the dangerous naïvety of idealism. Carr's form of "realism," however, amounted to a denial of idealism; it did not actually have much predictive power in itself. Morgenthau criticized Carr in an essay for being philosophically "ill-equipped," implying that he had no point of view outside of history "from which to survey the political scene and to appraise the phenomenon of power."[8]

In Morganthau's view, Carr had a lot of evidence but not much theoretical framework to tie it all together—the difference between reporting on the facts and understanding the forces that define the facts.

NOTES

1   Hans J. Morgenthau, *Politics Among Nations: The Struggle for Power and Peace*, 7th ed (New York: McGraw-Hill, 2006), 3.

2   Morgenthau, *Politics Among Nations*, 36.

3   Morgenthau, *Politics Among Nations*, 36.

4   Morgenthau*, Politics Among Nations*, 19.

5   Morgenthau*, Politics Among Nations*, 19.

6   Morgenthau, *Politics Among Nations*, 20.

7   Morgenthau, *Politics Among Nations*, 30.

8   Hans J. Morgenthau, "Review: The Political Science of E. H. Carr," *World Politics* 1, no. 1 (1948): 134.

SECTION 2
IDEAS

MAIN IDEAS

KEY POINTS

- "Interest defined as power" is the most important theme of *Politics Among Nations*.

- Although humans naturally desire to control others, moral and legal considerations can limit that desire.

- Morgenthau lays out his ideas clearly and logically; in the contemporary field of international relations* this scientific approach was novel.

Key Themes

Hans J. Morgenthau builds *Politics Among Nations: The Struggle for Power and Peace* around three key themes—power, human nature, and the national interest. The primary theme revolves around an investigation of power. Morgenthau seeks to understand both its nature and its limitations—how power *can* be used, and how it *should* be used.

How power can be used is essentially the "balance of power;"* how power should be used, in Morgenthau's view, relates to international law and morality—"the moral rules that people actually observe"[1] when making foreign policy decisions.

More than a half-century after Morgenthau wrote *Politics Among Nations*, the study of power still lies at the heart of international relations. Scholars still debate Morgenthau's ideas and use them in developing new theories. Morgenthau's idea of power includes multiple variables. In this book he explains why states must accumulate power, and how this can increase national security. Morgenthau defines "national interest" as the state's understanding of what it does in the international sphere, and why. For Morgenthau, power plays a

66 The main signpost that helps political realism to find its way through the landscape of international politics is the concept of interest defined in terms of power. This concept provides the link between reason trying to understand international politics and the facts to be understood. 99

Hans J. Morgenthau, *Politics Among Nations*

central role in defining national interest, largely because statesmen are human. And, as Morgenthau sees it, it is in the nature of humans to pursue power and domination over each other.

Exploring the Ideas

When Morgenthau speaks of power in general, he means "man's control over the minds and actions of other men."[2] But when he talks about political power, he refers "to the mutual relations of control among the holders of public authority and between the latter and the people at large."[3] In other words: power is not just a compulsion; it is a *relationship* between those with authority and those who follow them.[4] For Morgenthau, this relationship is based on control. "Whatever the material objectives of a foreign policy," he writes, referring to things such as the invasion of a neighboring state or a call for a trade embargo, "they always entail control of the actions of others through influence over their minds."[5]

States may be the main actors in international affairs, but humans wield the power and pursue the policies. So human nature is important to international relations.[6] Foreign policy actors—presidents, prime ministers, the heads of government departments, diplomats, military officers, and foreign agents—all share the same human nature. They are all affected by the desire to pursue power over others for its own sake, and as such are subject to what is described by the Latin term *animus dominandi*—roughly, "spirit of dominating."

Morgenthau believed that people's tendency "to dominate" others can be found at every level of human society, both in the international community of states and inside domestic borders. But when statesmen wield power in the international sphere, there is no cross-national, international police force to prevent them from seeking to enforce their will.

As Morgenthau saw it, the state's "national interest" is to increase its power, and to prevent others from gaining power over it. Statesmen want to control themselves, and others, and want to avoid being controlled by others. The nature of power, and humans' desire for power, ultimately explains why conflict remains the defining force in the history of international relations.

The realist* school of thought is not a cynical formula for statesmen seeking to dominate others but, rather, a guide to the realities of politics. For Morgenthau, the greatest virtue a statesman can have is pragmatism.* Understanding that states have opposing interests keeps foreign policy grounded in reality.

Language and Expression

Not complicated by jargon, *Politics Among Nations* is easy to read, suitable for both undergraduate and postgraduate studies, and remains relevant to modern scholarship despite the move towards a more scientific approach to the study of international relations from the 1970s onwards. The work is well organized, for the most part; ideas flow logically, with each chapter building on the previous material.

Only in the last four sections of the book—a case study in applying realism* to international politics—does Morgenthau deviate from his theoretical framework. In the earlier parts of the book, he described and analyzed; in these last four sections, he prescribes. Here he discusses the possibility of a world state in which borders—and the role of diplomacy—are secondary to a world government.[7]

Although Morgenthau was the first to apply empirical* methods to the analysis of international relations, making deductions from observable evidence, his approach has nevertheless been criticized for not being sufficiently scientific. It should be noted, of course, that there is a degree of subjectivity in theorizing about international relations. This is apparent in the last four sections of the book, where Morgenthau applies realist theory to international politics.

These last four sections do not read like an analysis of international relations. Instead they are closer to what is usually labeled as prescriptive social science—that is, social science that is not meant to describe and analyze phenomena, but, rather, to indicate the best course of action.

It can therefore be argued that if Morgenthau's language and expression do not change throughout *Politics Among Nations*, his intentions do. This might make it difficult for a less advanced reader to understand where objective analysis ends and subjective prescription begins.

NOTES

1 Hans J. Morgenthau, *Politics Among Nations: The Struggle for Power and Peace*, 7th ed. (New York: McGraw-Hill, 2005), 240.

2 Morgenthau, *Politics Among Nations*, 30.

3 Morgenthau, *Politics Among Nations*, 30.

4 Morgenthau, *Politics Among Nations*, 30.

5 Morgenthau, *Politics Among Nations*, 33–4.

6 Morgenthau, *Politics Among Nations*, 114.

7 Morgenthau, *Politics Among Nations*, 505–68.

SECONDARY IDEAS

KEY POINTS

- Morgenthau lays out how the fundamental theory of "interest defined as power" plays out in the real world.

- The main secondary ideas in the book are the emergence of "balance of power"* politics (that is, an international system in which power is distributed evenly), and the impossibility of finding peace through unity.

- Critics have generally overlooked Morgenthau's emphasis on the roles of law and morality in limiting power.

Other Ideas

Hans J. Morgenthau's *Politics Among Nations: The Struggle for Power and Peace* discusses complementary ideas related to the key themes of power, international law, and morality. He develops these ideas in the seventh to tenth parts of this work.[1] In these sections, he applies his theoretical framework to the post–World War II* world, looking at what "peace" means and, more importantly, how to achieve it.

Although, for Morgenthau, most states seek to maximize their power, which inevitably leads to war, morality nevertheless serves as a path toward peace. It is their morality that makes statesmen consider their behavior and accept that certain actions—disarmament, collective security, or the creation of a world government, for example—can create a peaceful environment.

Historical experience allows Morgenthau to discuss the difficulty of implementing these actions. States find it difficult to commit to disarmament, for example, never mind to implement it—a difficulty compounded by the onset of the nuclear age during World War II.

> ❝ [Realism], then, sees in a system of checks and balances a universal principle for all pluralist societies. It appeals to historical precedent rather than to abstract principles and aims at the realization of the lesser evil rather than the absolute good. ❞
>
> Hans J. Morgenthau, *Politics Among Nations*

Meanwhile, collective security is not enforceable in the absence of an international police force unbound by borders. As for the creation of a world government, the experience of the League of Nations* (the predecessor to the United Nations)* demonstrates the ease with which it can be challenged.

More importantly, Morgenthau recognizes a number of factors that impede world peace. Chief among them is the "national interest." As he sees it, when statesmen make decisions about war and peace, national interest often trumps moral considerations.

Exploring the Ideas

"Realism,"* Morgenthau argues, "considers prudence—the weighing of the consequences of alternative political actions—to be the supreme virtue in politics."[2] Recognizing this does not mean we approve of everything a nation wants to say or do. But it does allow us to lay bare the hypocrisy of nations that clothe their actions in moral language. Morgenthau notes that all nations are "tempted to clothe their own particular aspirations," meaning their quest for power, in "moral purposes."[3] So, in this formulation, if one nation intends to conquer another to spread its religion, its actual intent is just to extend its power. Politics, therefore, is "autonomous"—it is not the application of law, morality, or any other standard of thought (including economics). Its only relevant question is: "how does this policy affect the power of the nation?"[4]

Morgenthau is careful, however, not to deny that statesmen operate with some kind of morality.

"Viewed as a series of technical tasks into which moral considerations do not enter," he argues, even genocide—the complete extermination of a people—would be considered if it served the interests of state power.[5] Where are morals in international relations?* As Morgenthau sees it, they do not exist in the power politics* between states. Instead, moral feelings "operate within the consciences of individual men."[6] This is part of the complexity in international affairs that Morgenthau highlights: humans have, and often act on, moral feelings. But the *act of doing politics* is ultimately about power.

Morgenthau believes that although statesmen will do what they can inside the bounds of their morality, their ultimate actions only reflect what can be accomplished in the realm of power.

Overlooked

Although modern readers, especially students of international relations, may want to view Morgenthau as simply a theorist of power, he was much more.

He was, in fact, a theorist of the complex forces that define political action. The American professor of international affairs Robert Jervis* writes: "Many studies begin with a ritual assertion that realism, being deeply rooted in unchanging material interests, ignores the role of ideas."[7] Realism, in other words, is often seen—wrongly—as merely *describing* what exists, rather than having *ideas about what ought to be*. For all Morgenthau's focus on "interest defined as power," writes Jervis, he "clearly saw that statesmen can conceive of their interests in quite different ways."[8]

Nowhere is this more apparent than in Morgenthau's discussion of morality.

Explaining Morgenthau's concept of morality, Jervis writes that, "properly conceived, [it] seeks to both further the state's legitimate interests and respect those of others," and to recognize that while the state must protect itself, there can be common ground between positions.[9] Although Morgenthau does not present a precise theory of how to adjudicate between these two principles, this did not mean he believed moral feelings and moral commitments were irrelevant to international politics. He merely believed they were not the *primary driver* of international politics. Ultimately, this sensitivity to multiple drivers of state action reinvigorated interest in Morgenthau in the period following the Cold War.*

NOTES

1   Hans J. Morgenthau, *Politics Among Nations: The Struggle for Power and Peace*, 7th ed. (New York: McGraw-Hill, 2006), 337–568.

2   Morgenthau, *Politics Among Nations*, 12.

3   Morgenthau, *Politics Among Nations*, 12.

4   Morgenthau, *Politics Among Nations*, 13.

5   Morgenthau, *Politics Among Nations*, 241.

6   Morgenthau, *Politics Among Nations*, 257.

7   Robert Jervis, "Hans Morgenthau, Realism, and the Scientific Study of International Politics," *Social Research* 61, no. 1 (1994): 861.

8   Jervis, "Hans Morgenthau," 861.

9   Jervis, "Hans Morgenthau," 869.

ACHIEVEMENT

KEY POINTS

- Morgenthau's work was successful in developing a new theory of international relations*—but not necessarily in its application of the scientific method* (that is, by measuring evidence, testing a hypothesis, and so on).

- As the Cold War* brought with it a new era of international power politics,* the arguments made in *Politics Among Nations* continued to be relevant.

- Morgenthau's six principles of political realism* have been criticized as being androcentric (that is, prioritizing a male perspective). A feminist perspective offers different ideas of what power is and how it can be used.

Assessing the Argument

Hans J. Morgenthau's *Politics Among Nations: The Struggle for Power and Peace* successfully introduced a new theoretical model to understand international relations. He popularized a new theory—that of realism—whose principles are still in use more than 60 years after the book was published.

Morgenthau influenced the way we think about international politics by offering a clear case study to test the validity of his hypothesis, presented at the beginning of the work in the form of six principles.

Politics Among Nations did not introduce realism as a clear and testable theory, however, but as a way of seeing the world. Applying the scientific method requires collecting data to test a hypothesis. If the hypothesis is validated, other researchers would need to be able to

> ❝ The difference, then, between political realism and the other schools of thought is real, and it is profound. However much of the theory of political realism may have been misunderstood and misinterpreted, there is no gainsaying its distinctive intellectual and moral attitude to matters political. ❞
>
> Hans J. Morgenthau, *Politics Among Nations*

reproduce the test with different data. In the field of international relations, the scientific method could only successfully prove a hypothesis if the behavior of all actors grouped under one category ("great powers,"* for example) was the same under a particular circumstance (a war threat from another great power, for example). History proves that this is not the case.

Nevertheless, the book is currently in its seventh edition, so that way of seeing the world clearly remains compelling, even 60 years after it first appeared. His idea that states struggle for power in the form of relative gains* remains a popular explanation of international relations. Morgenthau may not have been the first thinker to make this argument, but he was the first to articulate its general principles clearly.

Achievement in Context

More than six decades after its publication, *Politics Among Nations* remains a central text of what we now call classical realism.* This term distinguishes Morgenthau's realism from its successors, such as neorealism,* also called structural realism* (according to which the structure of the international system decides the behavior of states); neoclassical realism* (according to which a state's behavior is decided by domestic perceptions of how power is distributed between nations);

and the English school* of international relations (according to which international institutions moderate the behavior of states in an otherwise anarchic* system).

These new schools of thought have updated Morgenthau's theory by building on concepts articulated in *Politics Among Nations*: an anarchical international system with no higher authority to keep the peace, the struggle for power among states, and state self-interest.

After World War II,* the Cold War complicated Morgenthau's position. The British international relations scholar Michael Cox* wrote that, "in the late 1940s … the Cold War began to assume an apparently permanent form," as both blocs became increasingly evenly matched.[1] Cox said Morgenthau believed America's "purpose in international affairs [was] to make sure [the Soviets] did not win" the Cold War.[2]

In the run-up to World War II, international relations involved a complex cast of characters, and a number of different states. In contrast to this, the Cold War was—or at least appeared to be—fairly simple. In effect, only two players mattered: the US and the Soviet Union.* This reduced complexity in the international arena led to a "behaviorist turn" in international relations—that is, scientific methodology became increasingly important in the analysis of international relations. As a result, Morgenthau enjoyed less influence as these more rigorously "scientific" theories of politics came to the fore.

After the Cold War, however, when the world became a more complex place, politically speaking, Morgenthau's theories began to attract interest once more.

As Morgenthau would have predicted, the collapse of the Soviet Union and the end of the Cold War did not signal an end to conflict. International relations, and realism in particular, remains just as important in light of the US-led invasions of Afghanistan* in 2001 and Iraq* in 2003. The American political historian Francis Fukuyama* had proclaimed the "end of history"* and the victory of liberal democracy* over communism* and fascism.*[3] But apparently the celebrations were premature. Actors—states or statesmen—with different ideologies will always emerge to challenge the dominant powers.

Limitations

Feminist scholars of international relations have provided one key criticism of Morgenthau's theory. They felt he could not claim to have derived his analysis from universal human nature because he had excluded at least half the population: women.

In her article "Hans Morgenthau's Principles of Political Realism: A Feminist Reformulation," the American international relations scholar J. Ann Tickner* criticized Morgenthau's theory as being "embedded in a masculine perspective."[4] She argued that while Morgenthau saw "power as domination," a female understanding of power emphasizes sharing, cooperation, and "acting together."[5] While Morgenthau saw the "national interest defined as power," Tickner saw it as "multidimensional" to the point that it could not "be defined solely in terms of power." Moreover, she adds, "In the contemporary world the national interest demands co-operative rather than zero-sum* solutions" (that is, solutions in which one's gains are another's losses) to global problems shared by everyone.[6]

Tickner aims to complete Morgenthau's theory, which she sees as only half-complete. To her, and to other feminist critics, it explains only one aspect of human interaction (masculine, founded on principles of domination and opposition). And it bases its ambitions for peace solely on taming this aspect. Tickner would explain all aspects of human nature—to see desire for power not as the tragedy of human life, but as a force with the potential to enable people to put aside petty differences.

NOTES

1   Michael Cox, "Hans J. Morgenthau, realism, and the rise and fall of the Cold War," in *Realism Reconsidered: The Legacy of Hans Morgenthau in International Relations*, ed. Michael C. Williams (Oxford: Oxford University Press, 2007), 169.

2   Cox, "Morgenthau and the Cold War," 169.

3   Francis Fukuyama, *The End of History and the Last Man* (New York: Free Press, 1992).

4   J. Ann Tickner, "Hans Morgenthau's Principles of Political Realism: A Feminist Reformulation," *Millennium: Journal of International Studies* 17, no. 3 (1988): 430.

5   Tickner, "Hans Morgenthau's Principles of Political Realism," 434.

6   Tickner, "Hans Morgenthau's Principles of Political Realism," 438.

MODULE 8
PLACE IN THE AUTHOR'S WORK

KEY POINTS

- *Politics Among Nations* was Morgenthau's second major work in English; his later work became less general and focused more on particular events.

- In his later career, Morgenthau focused on criticizing American foreign policy during the Cold War.*

- *Politics Among Nations* was one of the first books to offer a distinctive theory of international relations.* It has been republished seven times.

Positioning

Politics Among Nations: The Struggle for Power and Peace was Hans J. Morgenthau's second major work in English, and became his most famous. His first, published in 1946, was *Scientific Man Versus Power Politics*. It prefigured many of the most important points of *Politics Among Nations*, especially the importance of morality in international politics, the criticism of the approach to international relations known as liberalism* as unreasonably naïve, and the skepticism that politics could be studied like a natural science.

As the Cold War began, Morgenthau offered policy advice more directly applicable to the United States. In *In Defense of the National Interest* (1951), he criticized the American approach to its conflict with the Soviet Union.* He believed the US was too assured of its own victory in a conflict it was far from guaranteed to win. He extended this critique in 1960 in his book *The Purpose of American Politics*.

Over the course of the Cold War, Morgenthau focused more on writing articles than full-length books. As he became more widely

66 Not only did Morgenthau write two of postwar Realism's most influential books, *Politics Among Nations: The Struggle for Power and Peace* (1948) and *In Defense of the National Interest* (1951), but he penned about a dozen others, as well as hundreds of scholarly articles on an astonishing range of topics. Unlike most academics, Morgenthau also became a much sought-after public intellectual. 99

William E. Scheuerman, *Morgenthau*

known, he became less of a political theorist, writing in general about politics. Instead he fashioned himself as a critic of foreign policy, writing about particular political decisions at particular places and times. Many of his essays offered blunt criticisms of American foreign policy, as their titles indicate: "We Are Deluding Ourselves in Vietnam" (1965) or "US Misadventure in Vietnam" (1968). In the latter he argued that American policies in Vietnam "run counter to American interests … and the United States' objectives are not attainable … without unreasonable moral liabilities and material risks."[1] In other words, he believed the United States risked mistaking some general principle—that communism* ought to be fought all over the world—with its own national interests.

Integration

As Morgenthau became a foreign policy critic, the general prescriptions he offered in *Politics Among Nations* became more specific. In *In Defense of the National Interest* (1951) he reminds American foreign policy makers that they should not see their duty to spread democracy* as a grand service to the world but as merely an aspect of foreign policy. "Remember always," Morgenthau writes, "that it is not only a political necessity, but also a moral duty for a nation to always follow in its dealings with other nations but one guiding star [rather than] the crusading notion that any nation … can have the mission to make the world over in its own image."[2]

In *The Purpose of American Politics* (1960), Morgenthau continued to criticize American foreign policy for confusing its national interest (countering the Soviet threat) with its ideological commitment (spreading democracy). "In order to be worthy of our lasting sympathy," he writes, "a nation must pursue its interests for the sake of a transcendent purpose"—a goal that, going beyond mere survival, "gives meaning to the day-to-day operations of its foreign policy."[3]

Morgenthau's foreign policy prescriptions are not at odds with the theory he expressed in *Politics Among Nations*. He believed morality and the national interest were deeply entwined. And while he believed that nations must act morally, he recognized the tragic reality that often they do not. Morgenthau believed it was not just confusing but dangerous to confuse ideology and foreign policy. Of the war in Vietnam, he wrote that it was "ideologically consistent, but politically and militarily foolish to oppose a Communist government for no other reason than that it is Communist."[4] In Morgenthau's view the war in Vietnam was not only immoral; it was also a foreign policy error.

Significance

Politics Among Nations made Morgenthau one of the most influential scholars in international relations. Realism* remains one of the three key theoretical paradigms* used to study behavior in the international system, along with liberalism (an approach that holds that cooperation between nations is possible if states seek to achieve absolute gains* rather than relative gains),* and constructivism* (an approach to international relations that holds that interactions between states do not result from unchanging laws of human nature but are socially constructed, and can, therefore, be altered).

A 2012 survey of international relations scholars showed that at the undergraduate level a majority teaches more about realism than any other model.[5] It can also be estimated from responses to the survey that about a third of international relations literature uses realism[6] and that the approach was the second most common theoretical approach to the study of international politics by scholars in the field.[7] Thus, more than 60 years after the publication of *Politics Among Nations*, the theory it presents still informs the study and research of international politics.

Morgenthau created a new way to understand international politics and to analyze the foreign policy of states. With this book he influenced generations of international relations scholars—and, consequently, practitioners. *Politics Among Nations* remains one of the core texts in the field. It can be argued that in this book Morgenthau defined our understanding of interactions among states. He also presented a new way of approaching the study of international relations—using the scientific method* to try to present a coherent and testable argument. This method remains in frequent use throughout the discipline today.

NOTES

1 Hans J. Morgenthau, "US Misadventure in Vietnam," *Current History* 54, no. 317 (1968): 29. See also, Hans J. Morgenthau, "We Are Deluding Ourselves in Vietnam," *New York Times Magazine*, April 18, 1965.

2 Hans J. Morgenthau, *In Defense of the National Interest: A Critical Examination of American Foreign Policy* (New York: Knopf, 1951), 214–15.

3 Hans J. Morgenthau, *The Purpose of American Politics* (New York: Knopf, 1965), 8.

4 Hans J. Morgenthau, quoted in Lorenzo Zambernardi, "The Impotence of Power: Morgenthau's Critique of American Intervention in Vietnam," *Review of International Studies* 37, no. 3 (2011): 1341.

5 Daniel Maliniak et al., *TRIP around the World: Teaching, Research, and Policy Views of International Relations Faculty in 20 Countries* (Williamsburg, VA: Teaching, Research, and International Policy (TRIP) Project, 2012), 12.

6   Maliniak et al., *TRIP around the World*, 47.

7   Maliniak et al., *TRIP around the World*, 27.

SECTION 3
IMPACT

THE FIRST RESPONSES

KEY POINTS

- Critics claimed *Politics Among Nations* was both overly cynical about prospects for peace in international politics and insufficiently scientific.

- Morgenthau responded that the preconditions for peace did not exist in the international system, and that scientific analysis was too simplistic for the complex domain of international politics.

- The debate moved on to focus more on methodology (classical or scientific approaches) and less on outcomes (idealism* or realism*—approaches to international relations* with very different ideas about the possibility of peace between nations and different assumptions about the motivations of states).

Criticism

Although Hans J. Morgenthau's *Politics Among Nations: The Struggle for Power and Peace* quickly enshrined realism as the key school of thought in international relations during the Cold War* period, naturally the work had its critics. The Austrian American historian Frank Tannenbaum* believed that realism in foreign policy merely prolongs conflict. "It is possible and desirable," Tannenbaum argued, "if man wishes to save himself from destruction, to organize international relations on the basis of a coordinate state."[1] This argument corresponds to the approach to international relations known as idealism. In Tannenbaum's view, states retain domestic powers, but must subordinate themselves to an international system in which they settle foreign policy

❝ The fact that so erudite a scholar as Professor Hans J. Morgenthau, of the University of Chicago, and so subtle a mind as George F. Kennan are the chief proponents of this dreadful doctrine [realism] in the United States will add zest to the debate ... But the American people will not take this advice, for they cannot act upon it without ceasing to be both a Christian and a democratic people. ❞

Frank Tannenbaum, "The Balance of Power"

issues cooperatively. This comes very close to advocating a world state.

Tannenbaum criticized Morgenthau for accepting balance of power* politics as the baseline for international relations (that is, for his belief that the pursuit and distribution of power among nations is key to any analysis). He and other critics argued that Morgenthau was too cynical. He was unwilling to believe in the possibility of a foreign policy that drove to an ultimately moral end, and produced lasting peace among nations. Even Morgenthau's critics believed that in the absence of an authority to prevent them from fighting, states would fight. Although they disagreed with him, they were clearly influenced by Morgenthau's views.

The most strident criticisms of the work came not from a liberal counter-theory, but rather from other realists who found Morgenthau's theory insufficiently systematic. In his 1959 book *Man, the State, and War*, the American political scientist Kenneth Waltz*—whose work formed the basis of the neorealist* approach to international relations, arguing that the structure of the international system is key to any analysis—discusses some of the theoretical limitations of *Politics Among Nations*. In general, Waltz believed that theories such as Morgenthau's fell into the trap of "explaining nothing by trying to explain too much."[2]

By this, Waltz meant that Morgenthau tried to create a theory that would encompass all the complexities of international politics, from human nature, to morality, to different states. But such a broad theory cannot be useful in predicting future behavior. "The events of world history" cannot be separated from the people involved in them; "the importance of human nature" as the *main cause* of social events "is reduced by the fact that the same nature, however defined, has to explain an infinite variety of social events."[3]

Responses

Politics Among Nations has been reissued seven times. Morgenthau did not modify his core argument in subsequent editions in response to criticisms unless it was to further strengthen his position. In response to Tannebaum, for example, he discussed the possibility of the emergence of a superstate, referring to the way in which the Thirteen Colonies* had been transformed into the United States in the eighteenth century after they declared their independence from Britain and formed a union. However, whereas the colonies had a shared language and religion, there is not such common ground at the international level. In his article "Another Great Debate," Morgenthau writes that "it is not the disinterested coordination of facts" that has given rise to the utopian* theory of Tannenbaum, but, rather, "an emotional urge" to be optimistic.[4]

Morgenthau also used latter editions of *Politics Among Nations* to rebut Waltz's criticism that his realism was insufficiently scientific. *Politics Among Nations* contains Morgenthau's most strident argument against seeing international relations as a rigorous science. "The first lesson the student of international politics must learn and never forget," Morgenthau argues, "is that the complexities of international affairs make simple solutions and trustworthy prophecies impossible."[5] This was not a denial of the possibility of understanding the principles underlying politics. He viewed political action to be so complex that using these actions to predict future actions would require gross oversimplification. Scholars can understand fundamental truths about human nature, but, in Morgenthau's view, those truths will always be filtered through real circumstances and the actions of real people. Although we can understand them, we cannot predict them with the same reliability as we could, say, if we dropped an apple from a great height a dozen times to see if it would smash.

Conflict and Consensus

Did this debate between realism and idealism influence the understanding and importance of *Politics Among Nations*? To a large extent, it did not. By the time Morgenthau's work was published, the "Great Debate" had been going for over 20 years. Both sides had staked out their positions.

The next major shift in the discipline would not happen until the 1960s and 1970s, when the discipline of international relations became increasingly fragmented. When Morgenthau wrote *Politics Among Nations*, scholars were largely debating two opposing conclusions. But by the 1960s, the debate had grown to encompass many opposing methodologies. The traditional method of studying international relations was seen as little more than "descriptive history" or normative theory,* considered neither "explicit enough on its assumptions [nor] stringent enough about its hypothesis."[6]

This methodological debate remains relevant today. The American political scientist Morton Kaplan* and his Australian contemporary Hedley Bull* were two of the major players in the debate when it started during the 1960s. "In the United States," writes Bull, "the scientific approach has progressed from a fringe activity in the academic study of international relations [to the main methodological approach]." In Bull's view, scientific methodology* oversimplifies the complex world of international relations in such a way that it overstates "the degree of control and manipulation" that can be achieved in political action.[7]

NOTES

1   Frank Tannenbaum, "The Balance of Power Versus the Coordinate State," *Political Science Quaterly* 67, no. 2 (1952): 175.

2   Kenneth Waltz, "Realist Thought and Neorealist Theory," *Journal of International Affairs* 44, no. 1 (1990): 26.

3   Kenneth Waltz, *Man, the State, and War: A Theoretical Analysis* (New York: Columbia University Press, 1959), 27.

4   Hans J. Morgenthau, "Another 'Great Debate': The National Interest of the United States," *American Political Science Review* 4, no. 46 (1952): 968.

5   Hans J. Morgenthau, *Politics Among Nations: The Struggle for Power and Peace*, 7th ed. (New York: McGraw-Hill, 2006), 22.

6   Stefano Guzzini, *The Continuing Story of a Death Foretold: Realism in International Relations/International Political Economy* (Florence: European University Institute, 1992), 64.

7   Hedley Bull, "International Theory: The Case for a Classical Approach," *World Politics* 3, no. 18 (1966): 363.

THE EVOLVING DEBATE

KEY POINTS

- Realism* continued to be influential—even more so with the emergence in the 1990s of neoclassical realism,* which argues that the behavior of states is determined by perceptions of how power is balanced between them.

- Neoclassical realism is the most important contemporary school of thought to emerge from *Politics Among Nations.*

- Neorealism* (according to which the behavior of states can be explained by the structure of the international system), neoclassical realism, and the English school* (according to which morality and international institutions bring some structure to the anarchy* that otherwise defines international relations)* all have their roots in realism.

Uses and Problems

Hans J. Morgenthau's *Politics Among Nations: The Struggle for Power and Peace* represented the "classical approach" to international relations. But this approach became less fashionable as more scientific methodologies* emerged. The transformation of international relations can be understood as part of a "level of analysis problem," summed up by the American political scientist J. David Singer's* question "does one analyze the system, or the components of the system?"[1]

In 1979, the American political theorist Kenneth Waltz's* *Theory of International Politics*, a core text of neorealist thought, provided a decisive shift to the "system" level of analysis—that is, an analysis addressed to the superstructures of the international system itself.

> 66 International politics is the realm of power, of struggle, and of accommodation. The international realm is predominantly a political one ... The international realm [is variously described] as being anarchic, horizontal, decentralized, homogeneous, undirected, and mutually adaptive. 99
>
> Kenneth Waltz, *Theory of International Politics*

"It is not possible," Waltz argued, "to understand world politics simply by looking inside of states."[2] This, he believed, forced theorists "back to the descriptive level; and from simple descriptions no valid generalizations can logically be drawn."[3] Moreover, Waltz felt that the international system—particularly, its anarchic nature and the absence of a mechanism to keep states in line—was the source of conflict. This was because states all have the same goal—survival—and differ only in their ability to achieve that goal, considering things such as resources available to them, and so on.[4]

The problem with neorealism was that it could not predict change in the international system; it focused, above all else, on the dynamics of a bipolar* world order (that is, specifically, an international system defined by the two opposite "poles" of the Cold War:* the Soviet Union* and the United States). When the Cold War ended abruptly in the 1990s, it shocked international relations specialists.

Neoclassical realism then emerged in reaction to the inability of neorealism to explain the end of the Cold War. Neoclassical realism is a theory that accounts for both the power dynamics of the international system *and* the motives of the individual statesmen operating in it.

In his introduction to the book *International Relations Theory and the End of the Cold War*, the American political scientist Richard Ned

Lebow,* one of the earliest neoclassical realists, wrote that realists like Waltz "have depicted the Cold War as a bipolar security dilemma. Hans Morgenthau, the preeminent classical realist, on the other hand, viewed the Cold War as primarily an ideological struggle."[5]

Schools of Thought

Where Waltz wanted to avoid inventing a theory of foreign policy, believing it to be incidental to the real outcomes of international politics, neoclassical realists have sought to reconcile Morgenthau's realism with neorealism. They maintain that domestic variables—that is, differences inside states—have a significant impact on states' behavior. This is directly in line with Morgenthau's views. Modern theorists, however, also believe that structural factors shape state behavior.

Neoclassical realists aim to describe the interaction between state structure and foreign policy. The American political scientist Gideon Rose,* one of the key theorists of neoclassical realism, argues that "relative material power establishes the basic parameters of a country's foreign policy." This is the "neo" aspect of "neoclassical." However, Rose maintains, "foreign policy choices are maintained by actual political leaders and elites;" this is the "classical" aspect.[6]

Neoclassical realism, as outlined by Lebow, is ultimately more optimistic than classical realism:* "E. H. Carr* and Hans Morgenthau embraced realism in the dark decades of the 1930s and 1940s because it appeared to offer the best hope of saving humankind from the ravages of a new and more destructive war,"[7] he writes.

However, the end of the Cold War presented a different prospect from the end of World War II.* Contemporary realists, Lebow writes, "remain committed to the goal of peace." But he sees that "unduly pessimistic assumptions about the consequences of anarchy," and the assumption that states will always engage in conflicts "may now stand in the way of the better world we all seek."[8] In other words, the theory both Rose and Lebow describe offers greater flexibility to capture the complex multipolarity* (that is, the more distributed power) of the post-Cold War era.

In Current Scholarship

Unlike classical realism or neorealism, neoclassical realism does not have a center of key books, or a single set of consistent beliefs. It is more of an approach to international political theorizing than it is a clear theory. The American political scientist Randall Schweller* is one of the key theorists of neoclassical realism. He is currently modifying Waltz's theory of power balancing to account for what he calls "under balancing," which occurs when "threatened countries have failed to recognize a clear and present danger or, more typically, have simply not reacted to it or, more typically still, have responded in paltry and imprudent ways."[9]

Schweller looks to history for his evidence. He argues that "none of the great powers* (Britain, France, the United States, the Soviet Union, Italy, and Japan) balanced with any sense of urgency against Nazi* Germany." To counter the rising threat, he writes, they "bandwagoned,"* (aligned with more powerful nations), "buck-passed,"* (passed along any responsibility), "appeased" (gave in to demands or overlooked aggressions in the hope of peace), or "adopted ineffective half measures."[10]

In part, the great powers underestimated the threat of Nazi Germany; in part ,there was domestic political pressure to avoid confronting it. Waltz believes states will always respond rationally to threats. But Schweller notes that domestic politics can undermine rationality. He builds his analytic framework on "calculations of cost and risk" made by people in positions of power. These are defined by factors such as preferences and perceptions of the external environment, "personal" politics among people in powerful positions, and "the domestic political risks associated with certain foreign policy choices."[11]

NOTES

1   J. David Singer, "The Level-of-Analysis Problem in International Relations," *World Politics* 14, no. 1 (1961): 77.

2   Kenneth Waltz, *Theory of International Politics* (Addison Wesley: Reading, 1979), 64.

3   Waltz, *Theory of International Politics*, 64.

4   Waltz, *Theory of International Politics*, 121.

5   Richard Ned Lebow, introduction to *International Relations Theory and the End of the Cold War*, eds. Richard Ned Lebow and Thomas Risse-Kappen (New York: Columbia University Press, 1995), 16.

6   Gideon Rose, "Review: Neoclassical Realism and Theories of Foreign Policy," *World Politics* 51, no. 1 (1998): 146.

7   Richard Ned Lebow, "The Long Peace, the End of the Cold War, and the Failure of Realism," in *International Relations Theory and the End of the Cold War*, eds. Richard Ned Lebow and Thomas Risse-Kappen (New York: Columbia University Press, 1995), 50.

8   Lebow, "The Long Peace," 50.

9   Randall L. Schweller, "Unanswered Threats: A Neoclassical Realist Theory of Underbalancing," *International Security* 29, no. 2 (2004): 159.

10 Schweller, "Unanswered Threats," 160.

11 Schweller, "Unanswered Threats," 168–9.

MODULE 11
IMPACT AND INFLUENCE TODAY

KEY POINTS

- The modern rediscovery of Morgenthau's work has less to do with its focus on power politics* than its treatment of the roles of law and morality.

- Realism*—as exemplified in *Politics Among Nations*—has been challenged by constructivism,* which argues that the social qualities of a state have a great influence on its behavior.

- Neoclassical realist* theory, which has accommodated this constructivist idea, increasingly considers statesmen's ideas about their own interests.

Position

Hans J. Morgenthau's *Politics Among Nations: The Struggle for Power and Peace* may be even more relevant today than it was in the decades immediately following its publication. The Norwegian political scientist Torbjørn Knutsen* argues in his *History of International Relations Theory* that it is a "shallow misconception" to equate realism with "power politics," leaving aside moral feeling and individual choice.[1] His American contemporary, John A. Vasquez,* wrote that "*Politics Among Nations* … was so comprehensive, systematic, and theoretical, it became the exemplar [of realism]" and was the "single most important vehicle for establishing the dominance of the realist paradigm* in the field."[2]

Even after the Cold War* ended, Morgenthau's book continued to influence nearly every theorist. New theories emerged about the possibility of cooperation in international affairs, or the importance of

> ❝ Assumptions about motivation are necessary even in the most structural of theories. … The criticism is that [they do] not make clear that [their] conclusions about the effects of anarchy and the distribution of power depend on those assumptions. ❞
>
> Alexander Wendt, *Social Theory of International Politics*

states' identities in shaping their behavior. But these theories all recall Morgenthau's focus on power and his discussion of law and morality in particular.

Neoclassical realism has reinvigorated interest in Morgenthau's work, especially *Politics Among Nations*. Beginning in the 1990s, neoclassical realists sought to bring together neorealism's* emphasis on the importance of the international system and wider discussions about the role of ideas in the study of international relations.* This approach is similar to that of Morgenthau, who discussed power relations among states while stressing the importance of ideas about morality. Thus, neoclassical realism takes an approach very much like the one Morgenthau outlined in *Politics Among Nations*, reigniting debate on the work in the process.

Interaction

In the aftermath of the Cold War, debates in the field of international relations ranged beyond the simple opposition of realism and idealism.* Neoliberalism,* with its belief that states are concerned with achieving absolute gains* rather than relative gains,* emerged as a more economically focused version of idealism. Most importantly, neoliberalism and neorealism grew more similar to one another as theories of rational behavior. Constructivism also posed a methodological challenge; it holds that identity—the complex social history, forces, and systems that produce an "idea of the self" at the level of the state—primarily determines state behavior, and the international system is nothing but the product of the shared ideas of the states in it.

Morgenthau believed interest was defined as power. And Kenneth Waltz* believed interest was defined as security. But the German political scientist Alexander Wendt,* the most prominent constructivist thinker, argued that the international system was not fundamentally based on "power politics." He felt power politics was a social construct. In Wendt's view "identities are the basis of interest,"[3] meaning that every state has different interests defined by the way they think of themselves.

One state might consider itself the "leader of the free world," for example; another may see itself as an "imperial power."[4] Wendt imagines two theoretical states. Each wants to survive and has the means of its survival at its disposal, but neither has a particular incentive to conquer—or even to fear—the other. How the states interact will be based on a process of communication. If one state makes a peaceful gesture (believing cooperation to be safer than conflict), then relations between them will be peaceful.[5] It is through "reciprocal interaction"—actors acting and reacting to one another—that social structures are created "in terms of which we define our identities and interest."[6]

The Continuing Debate

Neoclassical realism has responded to the constructivist challenge largely by incorporating constructivist ideas. It sees itself as a kind of "middle way" between neorealism, which ignores the important role of ideas, and constructivism, which emphasizes them at the expense of a consideration of material facts and conditions such as resources and geography, and so on. As the scholar of international relations Gideon Rose* has discussed, neoclassical realism brings together elements of both neorealism and classical realism.* From neorealism, it gets an emphasis on the importance of material factors in determining the distribution of power in the international system. From classical realism, it accepts the fact that political leaders make decisions[7]—in other words, international affairs are conducted by human beings imposing their will on others.

Agreeing with Morgenthau, neoclassical realists believe that theory serves to understand decisions taken by statesmen.[8] This suggests the importance that ideas have for neoclassical realism. Using a neorealist theory, one has to analyze the distribution of power in the international system to understand the behavior of a state. In neoclassical realism, one also has to understand the ideas of its statesmen.

The American political scientist Jennifer Sterling-Folker* has examined the relations between China and Taiwan, combining identity analysis with neoclassical realism. Specifically, she asks "how is it possible for states that are engaged in an active security conflict to continue trading with one another?"[9] China has never recognized the sovereignty* of Taiwan, and yet the two countries have developed a close trading relationship. Each is, in effect, "trading with the enemy." Sterling-Folker sees Taiwan's national identity as constructed by "portraying China as an other against which a unified Taiwanese identity may be known … even as policymakers have encouraged greater economic linkages with China."[10]

The pursuit of trade is "secondary to the goal of maintaining this political separation from China."[11] In other words, even though the two states trade with one another, opposition to mainland China is a core part of the identity of Taiwan. National policy makers know this, and will continue to see China as a foe, regardless of the trade links.

NOTES

1   Torbjørn L. Knutsen, *A History of International Relations Theory* (Manchester: Manchester University Press, 1997), 243.

2   John A. Vasquez, *The Power of Power Politics: From Classical Realism to Neotraditionalism* (Cambridge: Cambridge University Press, 1999), 36.

3   Alexander Wendt, "Anarchy is what States Make of it: The Social Construction of Power Politics," *International Organization* 46, no. 2 (1992): 398.

4   Wendt, "Anarchy is what States Make of it," 398.

5   Wendt, "Anarchy is what States Make of it," 405.

6   Wendt, "Anarchy is what States Make of it," 406.

7   Gideon Rose, "Review: Neoclassical Realism and Theories of Foreign Policy," *World Politics* 51, no. 1 (1998): 146.

8   Rose, "Neoclassical Realism," 153.

9   Jennifer Sterling-Folker, "Neoclassical Realism and Identity: Peril Despite Profit Across the Taiwan Strait," in *Neoclassical Realism, the State, and Foreign Policy,* eds. Steven E. Lobell et al. (Cambridge: Cambridge University Press, 2009), 99.

10 Sterling-Folker, "Neoclassical Realism and Identity," 136.

11 Sterling-Folker, "Neoclassical Realism and Identity," 136.

WHERE NEXT?

KEY POINTS

- Morgenthau's theory is still being used as a basis for policy criticism—the American international relations* theorist John J. Mearsheimer* used the principles of *Politics Among Nations* to criticize the Iraq War.*

- Neoclassical realism* provides a useful framework to analyze the humbling of American power in the aftermath of the Cold War.*

- Morgenthau's book will likely remain a key text in international relations scholarship.

Potential

Hans J. Morgenthau's *Politics Among Nations: The Struggle for Power and Peace* will undoubtedly continue to be a key text in the field of international relations. Now in its seventh edition, it remains very influential in the era following 9/11*: the terrorist attacks of September 11, 2001. Leading international relations scholars have hailed it as a foundational text. Even today, the book evokes questions from leading scholars.

The American international relations theorist John J. Mearsheimer, who introduced the concept of offensive realism* in his influential 2001 book *The Tragedy of Great Power Politics*, recently asked, "Would Hans Morgenthau, the realist* who opposed going to war in Vietnam,* also have opposed the war on Iraq?"[1]

Mearsheimer sees right-wing neoconservative* politics, which aim to spread democracy,* by force if necessary, as similar to the idealism* Morgenthau opposed earlier in the twentieth century.

> ❝ The benefits to be had from transcending standard renditions of realism as being about crude inter-state power politics have recently been the subject of much debate. After having been proclaimed defunct at the beginning of the 1990s, efforts are now being undertaken to unearth the rich tradition of classical realism that has been lost to the scientific approach of subsequent structuralist, neo-realist approaches and the consequent fragmentation of the tradition. ... A number of other recent studies have also been exploring the value added of re-engaging with particular facets of classical realism, and Morgenthau is the common element throughout. ❞
>
> Oliver Jütersonke, *Morgenthau, Law and Realism*

Today's neoconservatives see the spread of democracy as a moral obligation.[2] Reaching back to Morgenthau, Mearsheimer argues that a state attempting to reshape the world by spreading its ideology is doomed to fail. He believes this because "the most powerful political ideology on the face of the earth is nationalism,* not democracy."[3] In contrast, realism recognizes that it is "terribly costly to invade and occupy countries ... in the developing world [that] believe fervently in self-determination, which is the essence of nationalism, and they do not like Americans or Europeans running their lives."[4] The closest parallel between Mearsheimer's criticism of the Iraq War and realism is Morgenthau's fifth principle: "political realism refuses to identify the moral aspirations of a particular nation with the moral laws that govern the universe."[5] This is the criticism of the American drive to spread its ideology around the world. The confusion of moral obligations and national interests remains as dangerous now as it was when Morgenthau wrote *Politics Among Nations* in 1948.

Future Directions

Kevin Marsh,* a young American international relations scholar, has suggested that neoclassical realism remains the best model for examining American national security strategy. In his article "Managing Relative Decline: A Neoclassical Realist Analysis of the 2012 US Defense Strategic Guidance," Marsh argued that neoclassical realism "responds both to the international balance of power* and the constraints imposed on American foreign policymaking by domestic politics and elite perceptions [that have led to a decline in relative power]."[6]

Marsh points to two domestic variables as two sources of this decline: "the [financial] crisis* and political gridlock plaguing the US." Among international variables he cites the fact that Iran may develop a nuclear weapon. He also notes the rise of China and the emergence of a multipolar* international order.[7] One of the most important constraints on foreign policy Marsh sees is fiscal, since "the United States simply could no longer afford open-ended annual increases in the defense budget," despite international threats.[8] Another critical constraint is domestic war-weariness: "The American people, tired of the bearing the cost and burden of Iraq and Afghanistan,"* support avoiding future conflict.[9] What is notable about the strategy is the increased reliance on "security cooperation" with international partners, rather than unilateral action.

In this way, a domestic factor has constrained the state's ability to respond to factors on the international level.

Summary

The American international relations scholars Kenneth W. Thompson* and W. David Clinton* write: "For most students of international relations, *Politics Among Nations* requires no introduction." In their view, the work has attained unquestioned status as "an intellectual staple for faculty and graduate students and for thousands of undergraduate students."[10] Hans Morgenthau's book is most often remembered for its maxim that nations pursue power over all else. But this is an oversimplification of what is, in fact, an extraordinarily complex work.

What sets Morgenthau's ideas apart is his belief that morality and international law limit the exercise of power. He shows how power lies at the center of realist thinking, and he was adamant that realism is the most appropriate theory with which to study international relations.

One of his views, however, remained uncommon for a long time: his acknowledgement that non-realist elements can be incorporated into a realist world view. In this sense, Morgenthau anticipated today's scholars who bring ideas from different traditions into his theory.

Politics Among Nations was one of the key texts that transformed the study of international relations into an accepted academic discipline. Morgenthau worked to bridge the gap between scholars and practitioners, creating a theory of international relations that could have a real-world application. He remains one of the most celebrated figures in the discipline, and is considered by many to be one of the founders of international relations.

NOTES

1   John J. Mearsheimer, "Hans Morgenthau and the Iraq War: Realism versus Neo-conservatism," *Open Democracy,* May 19, 2005, accessed April 13, 2015, https://www.opendemocracy.net/democracy-americanpower/morgenthau_2522.jsp.

2   Mearsheimer, "Morgenthau and the Iraq War."

3   Mearsheimer, "Morgenthau and the Iraq War."

4   Mearsheimer, "Morgenthau and the Iraq War."

5   Hans J. Morgenthau, *Politics Among Nations: The Struggle for Power and Peace,* 7th ed. (New York: McGraw-Hill, 2006), 12.

6   Kevin Marsh, "Managing Relative Decline: A Neoclassical Realist Analysis of the 2012 US Defense Strategic Guidance," *Contemporary Security Policy* 33, no. 3 (2012): 488.

7   Marsh, "Managing Relative Decline," 494.

8   Marsh, "Managing Relative Decline," 500.

9   Marsh, "Managing Relative Decline," 502.

10   Kenneth W. Thompson and W. David Clinton, preface to Hans J. Morgenthau, *Politics Among Nations: The Struggle for Power and Peace*, 7th ed (New York: McGraw-Hill, 2006), vi.

GLOSSARY

GLOSSARY OF TERMS

Absolute gain: a gain for a state (that is, an increase in power) that may also benefit another state. The liberal approach concentrates on the idea that it is important to make gains overall, not just over someone else.

Accommodation: the policy of attempting to reach a negotiated solution to a conflict between two or more actors (states or international institutions).

Afghan War: a military conflict that began in 2001 between a United States-led NATO coalition on the one side and Al-Qaeda and the Taliban on the other.

Anarchy: in international relations, the term "anarchy" refers to the absence of a central, organizing authority.

Anti-Semitism: discrimination or hatred directed towards Jewish people.

Balance of power: a distribution of power in the international system in which there is no dominant state in terms of military capabilities. It is a key realist concept, and one of the most debated in international relations.

Bandwagoning: a term describing what happens when a less powerful state aligns with another, more powerful, state to gain its protection.

Biopsychology: a branch of psychology studying the influence of the organism, especially the brain and the nervous system, in the behavior, thoughts, and feelings of human beings.

Bipolarity: in the international system, this refers to a distribution of power in which two states compete with one another. This competition influences the behavior of weaker states.

Buck-passing: the passing along of responsibility to another party.

Cold War (1947–91): a period of tension between the United States and its allies (often known as the "Western bloc") and the Soviet Union and its allies (often known as the "Eastern bloc.") The two powers avoided direct military conflict but carried out espionage and engaged in proxy wars (that is, sponsoring opposing sides in foreign conflicts).

Communism: roughly, a system of government following a socio-economic theory that shared ownership of the means of production (typically the resources and tools of industrial manufacturing) leads to a more a just, equal society.

Constructivism: one of the three most widely applied theoretical approaches to the study of international relations. Its key tenet is the belief that international relations are socially constructed. Therefore, interactions among actors are the result of the ways in which these actors understand themselves and others.

Containment: a policy adopted by the United States during the Cold War, which sought to contain the Soviet Union's perceived desires to expand through the establishment of a series of multilateral defense agreements.

Democracy: a system of government in which the ruler or rulers of a state are elected by the people, who can also participate in government through other channels such as referendums.

End of History: a reference to the influential essay of the same title by the American historian Francis Fukuyama, published in 1992, which claimed that a global turn towards democracies founded on the Western economic model heralded the end of international conflict.

Empirical: an approach to scientific analysis founded on deduction based on observable evidence.

English school of international relations: a theory of international relations first developed in the 1960s; at times considered as a form of realist theory and at times considered as a separate approach. It argues that even though the international system is anarchical, there is an international society based on common rules and institutions.

Fascism: an authoritarian system of government representing the absolute power of the central administration, and the dominance of the military and national industries.

Financial crisis: an economic recession in the early twenty-first century felt especially in the United States and Europe. It involved a severe crash in stock and debt markets around the world, constrained budgets, and rising unemployment.

Great power: in international relations, one of the most powerful countries at the international level.

Idealism: a theoretical approach to international relations that maintains that international politics can be defined by peace and cooperation if states seek to achieve relative gains rather than absolute gains.

Interdependence: when two states are interdependent, outcomes for either state depend (at least in part) on outcomes for the other state.

International relations: the branch of political science that studies the interactions between states, primarily foreign policies.

Iraq War (2003–11): an armed conflict between the United States and its allies and Iraq. After toppling the government of the dictator Saddam Hussein in 2003, the conflict descended into a sectarian civil war, which pitted Iraq's Shia and Sunni populations against each other. In December 2011, American forces withdrew from Iraq.

League of Nations: an international organization created in the aftermath of World War I. Its purpose was to promote international cooperation and multilateralism to prevent a new war involving the major world powers. However, one of its principles was to preserve the post-First World War status quo, and it was therefore challenged by Germany, Italy, and Japan in the 1930s. It ceased to exist in 1946.

Liberalism: a theory that argues that international politics can be defined by peace and cooperation if states seek to achieve absolute gains rather than relative gains. Throughout the Cold War, realism and liberalism (also known as liberal idealism) were the two main, opposing, theoretical models in international relations.

Multipolarity: a concept used to describe the distribution of power among a number of states. It stands in contrast to a bipolarity (two leading powers, or hegemons) and unipolarity (one hegemon).

Nationalism: a feeling of pride for one's country that often goes hand in hand with a sense of superiority over other countries.

Nazism: an extremely right-wing political movement that emerged in Germany following World War I. Its ideology was based on a strong military, corporate social organization, and aggressive nationalism. The Nazi government came to power in 1933, was one of the main antagonists at the outbreak of World War II in 1939, and was deposed by the Allied forces in 1945.

Neoclassical realism: a theory of international relations developed from the late 1990s onwards. The theory argues that state behavior is determined by domestic perceptions of the structure of power distribution in the international system.

Neoconservatism: a political ideology born in the United States, believing in the forceful promotion of free markets and democracy abroad.

Neoliberalism: a theory of international relations that maintains that state behavior is driven by absolute rather than relative gains.

Neorealism or structural realism: a theory of international relations first developed by Kenneth Waltz in *Theory of International Politics* (1979). The theory argues that state behavior is the result of the structure of the international system and the constraints it poses on its actors.

9/11: on September 11, 2001, politically radicalized Islamic terrorists hijacked four commercial airliners in the United States. The terrorists flew two into the twin towers of the World Trade Center in New York City, demolishing the buildings. They crashed a third plane into the Pentagon, a key building in the United States's military infrastructure. A fourth went down in a field in Pennsylvania. These coordinated attacks killed nearly 3,000 people.

Normative theory: Normative theory is a non-empirical statement of what ought to be, rather than what is. An example is: capital punishment should deter murder. An empirical argument, in contrast, would test this hypothesis to see whether or not it is true.

Offensive realism: a theory of international relations first put forward by John J. Mearsheimer that argues that aggressive behavior between states at an international level is a result of the lack of a central international authority.

Paradigm: a theoretical framework underlying the laws, practices, and thinking of a particular scientific subject.

Power politics: politics, especially at an international level, characterized by the use, or threat of, military or economic powers to achieve increased power or influence.

Pragmatism: an approach to beliefs or actions that values them in terms of outcomes.

Proxy war: a war instigated by a major power that does not itself become involved.

Raison d'état: literally, the "reason of state;" a political term referring to the national interest.

Realism (or classical realism): a theory of international relations that remains among the most used in the field. It is based on the idea that state behavior is driven by the self-interested accumulation of power to maximize relative gains.

Relative gain: in international relations, this would be a gain for one state in comparison with another. This realist approach follows the principle that there is a finite amount of power, so you can only get stronger if someone else gets weaker.

Scientific method: the process of accumulating knowledge by recognizing a problem, formulating a hypothesis to solve it, testing the hypothesis by collecting data through observation and experimentation, and validating the hypothesis. If the hypothesis cannot be validated, the entire process must start over again. This has been the standard method used in the natural sciences since the seventeenth century.

Sovereignty: the authority of a state to govern itself or another state.

Soviet Union, or USSR: a kind of "super state" that existed from 1922 to 1991, centered primarily on Russia and its neighbors in Eastern Europe and the northern half of Asia. It was the communist pole of the Cold War, with the United States as its main "rival."

Spanish Civil War (1936–9): a civil military conflict between republican forces (led by the democratically elected government) and Nationalist forces (led by General Francisco Franco). Franco's victory led to Spain becoming a military dictatorship until 1975.

Structural realism: another term for neorealism, a theory of international relations first developed by Kenneth Waltz in *Theory of International Politics* (1979). The theory argues that state behavior is the result of the structure of the international system and the constraints it poses on its actors.

Superpower: a very powerful and influential nation. This is a term often used to refer to the United States and the Soviet Union during the Cold War, when they were the two most powerful nations in the world.

Thirteen colonies (1607–1777): British colonies on the east coast of what is today the United States of America. People in these colonies rebelled against British control because although they were taxed, they were not represented in parliament. They became the United States in 1777, upon the adoption of Articles of Confederation—although the British did not recognize the new nation as a sovereign state until the end of the War of Independence in 1783.

United Nations: an intergovernmental organization representing (nearly) every state in the world. It is the main organization administering, among others, international health, development and security programs.

Utopia: an imagined place or state of things in which everything is perfect.

Vietnam War (1955–75): a two-decade-long military conflict between communist forces, led by North Vietnam, and anti-communist forces, led by the United States and South Vietnam. The war ended when American troops withdrew from Vietnamese territory in the face of great domestic opposition.

Western bloc: one of the two main groups of states during the Cold War, the other being the Eastern or Soviet bloc. The Western bloc was comprised of the United States, Western Europe, and other countries with a similar economic system in the Americas and the Asia-Pacific region.

Wilsonian: an adjective referring to the policies advocated by the US President Woodrow Wilson.

World War I (1914–18): a military conflict between the Allied forces, led by France, Italy, Russia, the United Kingdom, and (after 1917) the United States, and the Central powers, led by Austria-Hungary, Bulgaria, Germany, and the Ottoman Empire. The war left 16 million people dead.

World War II (1939–45): a military conflict between fascist forces, led by Germany, Italy, and Japan, and non-fascist forces, led by the Soviet Union, the United Kingdom, and (after 1940) the United States. It was the deadliest war in history, with over 60 million civilian and military casualties.

Zero sum: a situation in which whatever is gained by one side is lost by the other.

PEOPLE MENTIONED IN THE TEXT

Norman Angell (1872–1967) was an English economist, politician, and journalist. He is best known for his theory of interdependence, which states that countries that trade together are unlikely to fight, as it would not be to their material advantage.

Hedley Bull (1932–85) was a well-known international relations scholar. He is considered one of the founders of the English school of international relations; his book *The Anarchical Society* is a key text of that theoretical approach to international relations.

E. H. Carr (1892–1982) was an English historian, diplomat, journalist, and realist international relations theorist. He is best known for his work *The Twenty Years' Crisis 1919–1939: An Introduction to the Study of International Relations* (1939), which used the interwar period as a case study to explain how states behave toward one another. It contrasted realism with utopianism, and showed that states need realist policies in order to survive.

Michael Cox (b. 1947) is professor of international relations at the London School of Economics. He is currently co-director of the think tank LSE IDEAS.

W. David Clinton is an international relations scholar. He is best known as a leading voice of realism in international relations.

Francis Fukuyama (b. 1952) is a Japanese American professor of international relations at Stanford University. He is a well-known proponent of international liberalism, which refers to free markets, democratic elections, and Western secularism.

Martin Griffiths is an international relations academic currently working in Australia, whose interests include the history of the field of international relations from 1945.

Thomas Hobbes (1588–1679) was an English philosopher, best known as the author of *Leviathan*. He claimed that the state of nature of human beings is *bellum omnium contra omnes*—that is, war of all against all. This relates to realism's idea that the international system is anarchical in nature.

Robert Jervis (b. 1940) is a professor of international relations at Columbia University in the United States. He is most interested in the interplay between psychology, perception, and power structures.

Morton Kaplan (b. 1921) was professor of political science at the University of Chicago. He was one of the first theorists of international politics to focus on the structure of the international system.

George Kennan (1904–2005) was an American diplomat and academic. Ambassador to the Soviet Union in 1952, he is considered to be the founder of the policy of containment—seeking to limit the influence of the Soviet Union—that the United States implemented throughout most of the Cold War. As an academic, he was one of the greatest advocates of realism.

Robert O. Keohane (b. 1941) is an American political science professor at Princeton. He is associated with neoliberal institutionalism, and co-wrote its first book, *Power and Interdependence*, with Joseph Nye.

Torbjørn Knutsen (b. 1952) is a Norwegian theorist of international relations, focusing especially on the history of the discipline and its different methodologies.

Richard Ned Lebow (b. 1942) is an American political scientist who works in both America and the UK. He is considered to be among the first neoclassical realists.

Steven Lobell (b. 1964) is an international relations scholar. He is a well-known neoclassical realist,* having written several books using this theory.

Niccolò Machiavelli (1469–1527) was an Italian political philosopher and diplomat, best known as the author of *The Prince* in which he argued that the use of force and immoral behavior are sometimes necessary to retain power, since no means should be spared to achieve this end.

Halford Mackinder (1861–1947) was an English geographer. His geographical theory of politics was considered the first statement of what is now called "geopolitics."

Kevin Marsh is an academic at the University of Wooster in the United States, focusing on international relations theory in military affairs.

John J. Mearsheimer (b. 1947) is an international relations scholar and one of the best-known neorealists. His book *The Tragedy of Great Power Politics* is a key text of this theoretical approach.

Reinhold Niebuhr (1892–1971) was an American author and speaker. A devout Christian, he brought religious principles to international politics, rejecting the notion that liberal idealism should guide foreign policy. He supported military intervention and was a staunch anti-communist.

Gideon Rose (b. 1964) is an international relations scholar. One of the best-known neoclassical realists, he has been editor of *Foreign Affairs* since 2010.

Randall Schweller is professor of political science at the Ohio State University, where he has taught since 1994. He is one of the best-known neoclassical realist scholars in the field.

J. David Singer (1925–2009) was an American professor of political science. He is known for contributing to the "correlates of war" project, a long-term statistical project to determine the root causes of conflict.

Joseph Stalin (1878–1953) was leader of the Soviet Union as general secretary of the Communist Party from 1922 until his death in 1953. His brutal economic policies and political repression led to the deaths of millions. His successor, Nikita Khrushchev, denounced him as a tyrant.

Jennifer Sterling-Folker (b. 1960) is professor of international relations at the University of Connecticut. She specializes in theories of organization and governance.

J. Ann Tickner (b. 1937) is an American feminist theorist of international politics. She is best known for applying a "bottom up" analysis, breaking down existing assumptions popular in the discipline.

Frank Tannenbaum (1893–1969) was an Austrian American sociologist and advocate of labor rights. He specialized in criminal behavior and socialization.

Kenneth W. Thompson (1921–2013) was an international relations scholar and is one of the best-known realist scholars.

Thucydides (approximately 460–395 B.C.E.) was a Greek historian, best known for his *History of the Peloponnesian War*, a chronicle of the war between Athens and Sparta (431–404 B.C.E.). He is considered to be one of the first proponents of "realpolitik," the idea that in politics power and interests should take precedence over ideas and ethics.

John A. Vasquez (b. 1945) is professor of political science at the University of Illinois. He specializes in war, and how to classify and understand different wars.

Kenneth Waltz (1924–2013) was a key international relations scholar. The author of *Theory of International Politics* (1979), he is considered the founder of the neorealist approach to international relations. He also wrote *Man, the State, and War* (1959), in which he discussed three levels of analysis in the study of international politics: individual, state, and international system.

Alexander Wendt (b. 1958) is one of the key scholars in the field of international relations. He has been the main force leading constructivism to become one of the main theoretical approaches to the study of international politics since the 1990s. His main works are the article "Anarchy is what States Make of it: The Social Construction of Power Politics," published in 1992, and *Social Theory of International Politics*, published in 1999.

Woodrow Wilson (1856–1924) was the 28th president of the United States of America, in office from 1913 to 1921. Before entering politics, he was an academic—a professor of political science and president of Princeton University, one of the leading private universities in the US. He is best known for his liberal idealist principles and his role in building peace after World War I.

WORKS CITED

WORKS CITED

Angell, Norman. *The Great Illusion: A Study of the Relation of Military Power to National Advantage.* Project Gutenberg: Ebook, 2012.

Bull, Hedley. "International Theory: The Case for a Classical Approach." *World Politics* 18, no. 3 (1966): 361–77.

Carr, E. H. *The Twenty Years' Crisis, 1919–1939: An Introduction to the Study of International Relations.* New York: Harper and Row, 1964.

Cox, Michael. "Hans J. Morgenthau, realism and the rise and fall of the Cold War." In *Realism Reconsidered: The Legacy of Hans Morgenthau in International Relations*, edited by Michael C. Williams, 166–95. Oxford: Oxford University Press, 2007.

Frei, Christoph. *Hans J. Morgenthau: An Intellectual Biography.* Baton Rouge, LA: Louisiana State University Press, 2001.

Griffiths, Martin. *Fifty Key Thinkers in International Relations.* London: Routledge, 1999.

Guzzini, Stefano. *The Continuing Story of a Death Foretold: Realism in International Relations/International Political Economy.* Florence: European University Institute, 1992.

Hobbes, Thomas. *Leviathan.* Edited by J. C. A. Gaskin. Oxford: Oxford University Press, 1998.

Jervis, Robert. "Hans Morgenthau, Realism, and the Scientific Study of International Politics." *Social Research* 61, no. 1 (1994): 853–76.

Knutsen, Torbjørn L. *A History of International Relations Theory.* Manchester: Manchester University Press, 1997.

Lebow, Richard Ned. Introduction to *International Relations Theory and the End of the Cold War*, edited by Richard Ned Lebow and Thomas Risse-Kappen. New York: Columbia University Press, 1995.

Machiavelli, Niccolò. *The Prince.* Translated by Peter Bondanella. Oxford: Oxford World's Classics, 2005.

Mackinder, Halford. "The Geographical Pivot of History." *The Geographical Journal* 23, no. 4 (1904): 421–37.

Marsh, Kevin. "Managing Relative Decline: A Neoclassical Realist Analysis of the 2012 US Defense Strategic Guidance." *Contemporary Security Policy* 33, no. 3 (2012): 487–511.

McCormick, Thomas J. *America's Half-Century: United States Foreign Policy in the Cold War and After*. Baltimore: John Hopkins University Press, 1995.

Mearsheimer, John J. "Hans Morgenthau and the Iraq war: Realism versus Neo-conservatism." Accessed April 13, 2015. https://www.opendemocracy.net/democracy-americanpower/morgenthau_2522.jsp.

Morgenthau, Hans J. "Another 'Great Debate': The National Interest of the United States." *American Political Science Review* 46, no. 4 (1952): 961–88.

— — —. "Fragment of an Intellectual Biography." In *Truth and Tragedy: A Tribute to Hans. J. Morgenthau*, edited by. Kenneth W. Thompson and Robert J. Myers, 1–2. New Brunswick: Transaction Publishers, 1984.

— — —. *Human Rights and Foreign Policy*. New York: Council on Religion and International Affairs, 1979.

— — —. *In Defense of the National Interest: A Critical Examination of American Foreign Policy*. New York: Knopf, 1951.

— — —. "International Law and International Politics: An Easy Partnership." *Proceedings of the Annual Meetings of the American Society of International Law* (1974): 331–4.

— — —. "Law, Politics, and the United Nations." *Commercial Law Journal* 70, no. 1 (1965): 121–4.

— — —. *Politics Among Nations: The Struggle for Power and Peace*. 7th edition. New York: McGraw-Hill, 2006.

— — —. "Review: The Political Science of E. H. Carr." *World Politics* 1, no. 1 (1948): 127–34.

— — —. *Scientific Man versus Power Politics*. Chicago: University of Chicago Press, 1974.

— — —. *The Purpose of American Politics*. New York: Knopf, 1965.

— — —. "US Misadventure in Vietnam." *Current History* 54, no. 317 (1968): 29–34.

— — —. "We Are Deluding Ourselves in Vietnam" *New York Times Magazine*, April 18, 1965.

Niebuhr, Reinhold. *Man's Nature and His Communities: Essays on the Dynamics and Enigmas of Man's Personal and Social Existence*. New York: Charles Scribner's Sons, 1965.

— — —. *Moral Man and Immoral Society*. New York: Charles Scribner's Sons, 1932.

Rose, Gideon. "Review: Neoclassical Realism and Theories of Foreign Policy." *World Politics* 51, no. 1 (1998): 144–72.

Scheuerman, William E. *Morgenthau*. Cambridge: Polity Press, 2009.

Schmidt, Brian. Introduction to *International Relations and the First Great Debate*, edited by Brian Schmidt, 1–16. London: Routledge, 2012.

Schweller, Randall L. "Unanswered Threats: A Neoclassical Realist Theory of Underbalancing." *International Security* 29, no. 2 (2004): 159–201.

Singer, J. David. "The Level-of-Analysis Problem in International Relations." *World Politics* 14, no. 1 (1961): 77–92.

Sterling-Folker, Jennifer. "Neoclassical Realism and Identity: Peril Despite Profit Across the Taiwan Strait." In *Neoclassical Realism, the State, and Foreign Policy*, edited by Steven E. Lobell, Norrin M. Ripsman, and Jeffrey L. Taliaferro, 99–138. Cambridge: Cambridge University Press, 2009.

Tannenbaum, Frank. "The Balance of Power Versus the Coördinate State." *Political Science Quaterly* 67, no. 2 (1952): 173–97.

Thucydides. *The Peloponnesian War*. Translated by Martin Hammond. Oxford: Oxford University Press, 2009.

Tickner, J. Ann. "Hans Morgenthau's Principles of Political Realism: A Feminist Reformulation." *Millennium: Journal of International Studies* 17, no. 3 (1988): 429–40.

Vasquez, John A. *The Power of Power Politics: From Classical Realism to Neotraditionalism*. Cambridge: Cambridge University Press, 1999.

Waltz, Kenneth. *Man, the State, and War: A Theoretical Analysis.* New York: Columbia University Press, 1959.

— — —. "Realist Thought and Neorealist Theory." *Journal of International Affairs* 44, no. 1 (1990): 21–37.

— — —. *Theory of International Politics*. New York: McGraw Hill, 1979.

Wendt, Alexander. "Anarchy is what States Make of it: The Social Construction of Power Politics." *International Organization* 46, no. 2 (1992): 391–425.

— — —. *Social Theory of International Politics*. Cambridge: Cambridge University Press, 1999.

Wilson, Woodrow. "President Wilson's Message to Congress, January 8, 1918." Accessed April 8, 2015. http://www.ourdocuments.gov/doc.php?flash=true&doc=62.

X. "The Sources of Soviet Conduct." *Foreign Affairs* 65, no. 4 (1987): 566–82.

Zambernardi, Lorenzo. "The Impotence of Power: Morgenthau's Critique of American Intervention in Vietnam." *Review of International Studies* 37, no. 3 (2011): 1335–56.

THE MACAT LIBRARY
BY DISCIPLINE

The Macat Library By Discipline

AFRICANA STUDIES

Chinua Achebe's *An Image of Africa: Racism in Conrad's Heart of Darkness*
W. E. B. Du Bois's *The Souls of Black Folk*
Zora Neale Huston's *Characteristics of Negro Expression*
Martin Luther King Jr's *Why We Can't Wait*
Toni Morrison's *Playing in the Dark: Whiteness in the American Literary Imagination*

ANTHROPOLOGY

Arjun Appadurai's *Modernity at Large: Cultural Dimensions of Globalisation*
Philippe Ariès's *Centuries of Childhood*
Franz Boas's *Race, Language and Culture*
Kim Chan & Renée Mauborgne's *Blue Ocean Strategy*
Jared Diamond's *Guns, Germs & Steel: the Fate of Human Societies*
Jared Diamond's *Collapse: How Societies Choose to Fail or Survive*
E. E. Evans-Pritchard's *Witchcraft, Oracles and Magic Among the Azande*
James Ferguson's *The Anti-Politics Machine*
Clifford Geertz's *The Interpretation of Cultures*
David Graeber's *Debt: the First 5000 Years*
Karen Ho's *Liquidated: An Ethnography of Wall Street*
Geert Hofstede's *Culture's Consequences: Comparing Values, Behaviors, Institutes and Organizations across Nations*
Claude Lévi-Strauss's *Structural Anthropology*
Jay Macleod's *Ain't No Makin' It: Aspirations and Attainment in a Low-Income Neighborhood*
Saba Mahmood's *The Politics of Piety: The Islamic Revival and the Feminist Subjec*t
Marcel Mauss's *The Gift*

BUSINESS

Jean Lave & Etienne Wenger's *Situated Learning*
Theodore Levitt's *Marketing Myopia*
Burton G. Malkiel's *A Random Walk Down Wall Street*
Douglas McGregor's *The Human Side of Enterprise*
Michael Porter's *Competitive Strategy: Creating and Sustaining Superior Performance*
John Kotter's *Leading Change*
C. K. Prahalad & Gary Hamel's *The Core Competence of the Corporation*

CRIMINOLOGY

Michelle Alexander's *The New Jim Crow: Mass Incarceration in the Age of Colorblindness*
Michael R. Gottfredson & Travis Hirschi's *A General Theory of Crime*
Richard Herrnstein & Charles A. Murray's *The Bell Curve: Intelligence and Class Structure in American Life*
Elizabeth Loftus's *Eyewitness Testimony*
Jay Macleod's *Ain't No Makin' It: Aspirations and Attainment in a Low-Income Neighborhood*
Philip Zimbardo's *The Lucifer Effect*

ECONOMICS

Janet Abu-Lughod's *Before European Hegemony*
Ha-Joon Chang's *Kicking Away the Ladder*
David Brion Davis's *The Problem of Slavery in the Age of Revolution*
Milton Friedman's *The Role of Monetary Policy*
Milton Friedman's *Capitalism and Freedom*
David Graeber's *Debt: the First 5000 Years*
Friedrich Hayek's *The Road to Serfdom*
Karen Ho's *Liquidated: An Ethnography of Wall Street*

The Macat Library By Discipline

John Maynard Keynes's *The General Theory of Employment, Interest and Money*
Charles P. Kindleberger's *Manias, Panics and Crashes*
Robert Lucas's *Why Doesn't Capital Flow from Rich to Poor Countries?*
Burton G. Malkiel's *A Random Walk Down Wall Street*
Thomas Robert Malthus's *An Essay on the Principle of Population*
Karl Marx's *Capital*
Thomas Piketty's *Capital in the Twenty-First Century*
Amartya Sen's *Development as Freedom*
Adam Smith's *The Wealth of Nations*
Nassim Nicholas Taleb's *The Black Swan: The Impact of the Highly Improbable*
Amos Tversky's & Daniel Kahneman's *Judgment under Uncertainty: Heuristics and Biases*
Mahbub Ul Haq's *Reflections on Human Development*
Max Weber's *The Protestant Ethic and the Spirit of Capitalism*

FEMINISM AND GENDER STUDIES

Judith Butler's *Gender Trouble*
Simone De Beauvoir's *The Second Sex*
Michel Foucault's *History of Sexuality*
Betty Friedan's *The Feminine Mystique*
Saba Mahmood's *The Politics of Piety: The Islamic Revival and the Feminist Subject*
Joan Wallach Scott's *Gender and the Politics of History*
Mary Wollstonecraft's *A Vindication of the Rights of Woman*
Virginia Woolf's *A Room of One's Own*

GEOGRAPHY

The Brundtland Report's *Our Common Future*
Rachel Carson's *Silent Spring*
Charles Darwin's *On the Origin of Species*
James Ferguson's *The Anti-Politics Machine*
Jane Jacobs's *The Death and Life of Great American Cities*
James Lovelock's *Gaia: A New Look at Life on Earth*
Amartya Sen's *Development as Freedom*
Mathis Wackernagel & William Rees's *Our Ecological Footprint*

HISTORY

Janet Abu-Lughod's *Before European Hegemony*
Benedict Anderson's *Imagined Communities*
Bernard Bailyn's *The Ideological Origins of the American Revolution*
Hanna Batatu's *The Old Social Classes And The Revolutionary Movements Of Iraq*
Christopher Browning's *Ordinary Men: Reserve Police Batallion 101 and the Final Solution in Poland*
Edmund Burke's *Reflections on the Revolution in France*
William Cronon's *Nature's Metropolis: Chicago And The Great West*
Alfred W. Crosby's *The Columbian Exchange*
Hamid Dabashi's *Iran: A People Interrupted*
David Brion Davis's *The Problem of Slavery in the Age of Revolution*
Nathalie Zemon Davis's *The Return of Martin Guerre*
Jared Diamond's *Guns, Germs & Steel: the Fate of Human Societies*
Frank Dikotter's *Mao's Great Famine*
John W Dower's *War Without Mercy: Race And Power In The Pacific War*
W. E. B. Du Bois's *The Souls of Black Folk*
Richard J. Evans's *In Defence of History*
Lucien Febvre's *The Problem of Unbelief in the 16th Century*
Sheila Fitzpatrick's *Everyday Stalinism*

Eric Foner's *Reconstruction: America's Unfinished Revolution, 1863-1877*
Michel Foucault's *Discipline and Punish*
Michel Foucault's *History of Sexuality*
Francis Fukuyama's *The End of History and the Last Man*
John Lewis Gaddis's *We Now Know: Rethinking Cold War History*
Ernest Gellner's *Nations and Nationalism*
Eugene Genovese's *Roll, Jordan, Roll: The World the Slaves Made*
Carlo Ginzburg's *The Night Battles*
Daniel Goldhagen's *Hitler's Willing Executioners*
Jack Goldstone's *Revolution and Rebellion in the Early Modern World*
Antonio Gramsci's *The Prison Notebooks*
Alexander Hamilton, John Jay & James Madison's *The Federalist Papers*
Christopher Hill's *The World Turned Upside Down*
Carole Hillenbrand's *The Crusades: Islamic Perspectives*
Thomas Hobbes's *Leviathan*
Eric Hobsbawm's *The Age Of Revolution*
John A. Hobson's *Imperialism: A Study*
Albert Hourani's *History of the Arab Peoples*
Samuel P. Huntington's *The Clash of Civilizations and the Remaking of World Order*
C. L. R. James's *The Black Jacobins*
Tony Judt's *Postwar: A History of Europe Since 1945*
Ernst Kantorowicz's *The King's Two Bodies: A Study in Medieval Political Theology*
Paul Kennedy's *The Rise and Fall of the Great Powers*
Ian Kershaw's *The "Hitler Myth": Image and Reality in the Third Reich*
John Maynard Keynes's *The General Theory of Employment, Interest and Money*
Charles P. Kindleberger's *Manias, Panics and Crashes*
Martin Luther King Jr's *Why We Can't Wait*
Henry Kissinger's *World Order: Reflections on the Character of Nations and the Course of History*
Thomas Kuhn's *The Structure of Scientific Revolutions*
Georges Lefebvre's *The Coming of the French Revolution*
John Locke's *Two Treatises of Government*
Niccolò Machiavelli's *The Prince*
Thomas Robert Malthus's *An Essay on the Principle of Population*
Mahmood Mamdani's *Citizen and Subject: Contemporary Africa And The Legacy Of Late Colonialism*
Karl Marx's *Capital*
Stanley Milgram's *Obedience to Authority*
John Stuart Mill's *On Liberty*
Thomas Paine's *Common Sense*
Thomas Paine's *Rights of Man*
Geoffrey Parker's *Global Crisis: War, Climate Change and Catastrophe in the Seventeenth Century*
Jonathan Riley-Smith's *The First Crusade and the Idea of Crusading*
Jean-Jacques Rousseau's *The Social Contract*
Joan Wallach Scott's *Gender and the Politics of History*
Theda Skocpol's *States and Social Revolutions*
Adam Smith's *The Wealth of Nations*
Timothy Snyder's *Bloodlands: Europe Between Hitler and Stalin*
Sun Tzu's *The Art of War*
Keith Thomas's *Religion and the Decline of Magic*
Thucydides's *The History of the Peloponnesian War*
Frederick Jackson Turner's *The Significance of the Frontier in American History*
Odd Arne Westad's *The Global Cold War: Third World Interventions And The Making Of Our Times*

The Macat Library By Discipline

LITERATURE

Chinua Achebe's *An Image of Africa: Racism in Conrad's Heart of Darkness*
Roland Barthes's *Mythologies*
Homi K. Bhabha's *The Location of Culture*
Judith Butler's *Gender Trouble*
Simone De Beauvoir's *The Second Sex*
Ferdinand De Saussure's *Course in General Linguistics*
T. S. Eliot's *The Sacred Wood: Essays on Poetry and Criticism*
Zora Neale Huston's *Characteristics of Negro Expression*
Toni Morrison's *Playing in the Dark: Whiteness in the American Literary Imagination*
Edward Said's *Orientalism*
Gayatri Chakravorty Spivak's *Can the Subaltern Speak?*
Mary Wollstonecraft's *A Vindication of the Rights of Women*
Virginia Woolf's *A Room of One's Own*

PHILOSOPHY

Elizabeth Anscombe's *Modern Moral Philosophy*
Hannah Arendt's *The Human Condition*
Aristotle's *Metaphysics*
Aristotle's *Nicomachean Ethics*
Edmund Gettier's *Is Justified True Belief Knowledge?*
Georg Wilhelm Friedrich Hegel's *Phenomenology of Spirit*
David Hume's *Dialogues Concerning Natural Religion*
David Hume's *The Enquiry for Human Understanding*
Immanuel Kant's *Religion within the Boundaries of Mere Reason*
Immanuel Kant's *Critique of Pure Reason*
Søren Kierkegaard's *The Sickness Unto Death*
Søren Kierkegaard's *Fear and Trembling*
C. S. Lewis's *The Abolition of Man*
Alasdair MacIntyre's *After Virtue*
Marcus Aurelius's *Meditations*
Friedrich Nietzsche's *On the Genealogy of Morality*
Friedrich Nietzsche's *Beyond Good and Evil*
Plato's *Republic*
Plato's *Symposium*
Jean-Jacques Rousseau's *The Social Contract*
Gilbert Ryle's *The Concept of Mind*
Baruch Spinoza's *Ethics*
Sun Tzu's *The Art of War*
Ludwig Wittgenstein's *Philosophical Investigations*

POLITICS

Benedict Anderson's *Imagined Communities*
Aristotle's *Politics*
Bernard Bailyn's *The Ideological Origins of the American Revolution*
Edmund Burke's *Reflections on the Revolution in France*
John C. Calhoun's *A Disquisition on Government*
Ha-Joon Chang's *Kicking Away the Ladder*
Hamid Dabashi's *Iran: A People Interrupted*
Hamid Dabashi's *Theology of Discontent: The Ideological Foundation of the Islamic Revolution in Iran*
Robert Dahl's *Democracy and its Critics*
Robert Dahl's *Who Governs?*
David Brion Davis's *The Problem of Slavery in the Age of Revolution*

Alexis De Tocqueville's *Democracy in America*
James Ferguson's *The Anti-Politics Machine*
Frank Dikotter's *Mao's Great Famine*
Sheila Fitzpatrick's *Everyday Stalinism*
Eric Foner's *Reconstruction: America's Unfinished Revolution, 1863-1877*
Milton Friedman's *Capitalism and Freedom*
Francis Fukuyama's *The End of History and the Last Man*
John Lewis Gaddis's *We Now Know: Rethinking Cold War History*
Ernest Gellner's *Nations and Nationalism*
David Graeber's *Debt: the First 5000 Years*
Antonio Gramsci's *The Prison Notebooks*
Alexander Hamilton, John Jay & James Madison's *The Federalist Papers*
Friedrich Hayek's *The Road to Serfdom*
Christopher Hill's *The World Turned Upside Down*
Thomas Hobbes's *Leviathan*
John A. Hobson's *Imperialism: A Study*
Samuel P. Huntington's *The Clash of Civilizations and the Remaking of World Order*
Tony Judt's *Postwar: A History of Europe Since 1945*
David C. Kang's *China Rising: Peace, Power and Order in East Asia*
Paul Kennedy's *The Rise and Fall of Great Powers*
Robert Keohane's *After Hegemony*
Martin Luther King Jr.'s *Why We Can't Wait*
Henry Kissinger's *World Order: Reflections on the Character of Nations and the Course of History*
John Locke's *Two Treatises of Government*
Niccolò Machiavelli's *The Prince*
Thomas Robert Malthus's *An Essay on the Principle of Population*
Mahmood Mamdani's *Citizen and Subject: Contemporary Africa And The Legacy Of Late Colonialism*
Karl Marx's *Capital*
John Stuart Mill's *On Liberty*
John Stuart Mill's *Utilitarianism*
Hans Morgenthau's *Politics Among Nations*
Thomas Paine's *Common Sense*
Thomas Paine's *Rights of Man*
Thomas Piketty's *Capital in the Twenty-First Century*
Robert D. Putman's *Bowling Alone*
John Rawls's *Theory of Justice*
Jean-Jacques Rousseau's *The Social Contract*
Theda Skocpol's *States and Social Revolutions*
Adam Smith's *The Wealth of Nations*
Sun Tzu's *The Art of War*
Henry David Thoreau's *Civil Disobedience*
Thucydides's *The History of the Peloponnesian War*
Kenneth Waltz's *Theory of International Politics*
Max Weber's *Politics as a Vocation*
Odd Arne Westad's *The Global Cold War: Third World Interventions And The Making Of Our Times*

POSTCOLONIAL STUDIES

Roland Barthes's *Mythologies*
Frantz Fanon's *Black Skin, White Masks*
Homi K. Bhabha's *The Location of Culture*
Gustavo Gutiérrez's *A Theology of Liberation*
Edward Said's *Orientalism*
Gayatri Chakravorty Spivak's *Can the Subaltern Speak?*

The Macat Library By Discipline

PSYCHOLOGY

Gordon Allport's *The Nature of Prejudice*
Alan Baddeley & Graham Hitch's *Aggression: A Social Learning Analysis*
Albert Bandura's *Aggression: A Social Learning Analysis*
Leon Festinger's *A Theory of Cognitive Dissonance*
Sigmund Freud's *The Interpretation of Dreams*
Betty Friedan's *The Feminine Mystique*
Michael R. Gottfredson & Travis Hirschi's *A General Theory of Crime*
Eric Hoffer's *The True Believer: Thoughts on the Nature of Mass Movements*
William James's *Principles of Psychology*
Elizabeth Loftus's *Eyewitness Testimony*
A. H. Maslow's *A Theory of Human Motivation*
Stanley Milgram's *Obedience to Authority*
Steven Pinker's *The Better Angels of Our Nature*
Oliver Sacks's *The Man Who Mistook His Wife For a Hat*
Richard Thaler & Cass Sunstein's *Nudge: Improving Decisions About Health, Wealth and Happiness*
Amos Tversky's *Judgment under Uncertainty: Heuristics and Biases*
Philip Zimbardo's *The Lucifer Effect*

SCIENCE

Rachel Carson's *Silent Spring*
William Cronon's *Nature's Metropolis: Chicago And The Great West*
Alfred W. Crosby's *The Columbian Exchange*
Charles Darwin's *On the Origin of Species*
Richard Dawkin's *The Selfish Gene*
Thomas Kuhn's *The Structure of Scientific Revolutions*
Geoffrey Parker's *Global Crisis: War, Climate Change and Catastrophe in the Seventeenth Century*
Mathis Wackernagel & William Rees's *Our Ecological Footprint*

SOCIOLOGY

Michelle Alexander's *The New Jim Crow: Mass Incarceration in the Age of Colorblindness*
Gordon Allport's *The Nature of Prejudice*
Albert Bandura's *Aggression: A Social Learning Analysis*
Hanna Batatu's *The Old Social Classes And The Revolutionary Movements Of Iraq*
Ha-Joon Chang's *Kicking Away the Ladder*
W. E. B. Du Bois's *The Souls of Black Folk*
Émile Durkheim's *On Suicide*
Frantz Fanon's *Black Skin, White Masks*
Frantz Fanon's *The Wretched of the Earth*
Eric Foner's *Reconstruction: America's Unfinished Revolution, 1863-1877*
Eugene Genovese's *Roll, Jordan, Roll: The World the Slaves Made*
Jack Goldstone's *Revolution and Rebellion in the Early Modern World*
Antonio Gramsci's *The Prison Notebooks*
Richard Herrnstein & Charles A Murray's *The Bell Curve: Intelligence and Class Structure in American Life*
Eric Hoffer's *The True Believer: Thoughts on the Nature of Mass Movements*
Jane Jacobs's *The Death and Life of Great American Cities*
Robert Lucas's *Why Doesn't Capital Flow from Rich to Poor Countries?*
Jay Macleod's *Ain't No Makin' It: Aspirations and Attainment in a Low Income Neighborhood*
Elaine May's *Homeward Bound: American Families in the Cold War Era*
Douglas McGregor's *The Human Side of Enterprise*
C. Wright Mills's *The Sociological Imagination*

Thomas Piketty's *Capital in the Twenty-First Century*
Robert D. Putman's *Bowling Alone*
David Riesman's *The Lonely Crowd: A Study of the Changing American Character*
Edward Said's *Orientalism*
Joan Wallach Scott's *Gender and the Politics of History*
Theda Skocpol's *States and Social Revolutions*
Max Weber's *The Protestant Ethic and the Spirit of Capitalism*

THEOLOGY

Augustine's *Confessions*
Benedict's *Rule of St Benedict*
Gustavo Gutiérrez's *A Theology of Liberation*
Carole Hillenbrand's *The Crusades: Islamic Perspectives*
David Hume's *Dialogues Concerning Natural Religion*
Immanuel Kant's *Religion within the Boundaries of Mere Reason*
Ernst Kantorowicz's *The King's Two Bodies: A Study in Medieval Political Theology*
Søren Kierkegaard's *The Sickness Unto Death*
C. S. Lewis's *The Abolition of Man*
Saba Mahmood's *The Politics of Piety: The Islamic Revival and the Feminist Subject*
Baruch Spinoza's *Ethics*
Keith Thomas's *Religion and the Decline of Magic*

COMING SOON

Chris Argyris's *The Individual and the Organisation*
Seyla Benhabib's *The Rights of Others*
Walter Benjamin's *The Work Of Art in the Age of Mechanical Reproduction*
John Berger's *Ways of Seeing*
Pierre Bourdieu's *Outline of a Theory of Practice*
Mary Douglas's *Purity and Danger*
Roland Dworkin's *Taking Rights Seriously*
James G. March's *Exploration and Exploitation in Organisational Learning*
Ikujiro Nonaka's *A Dynamic Theory of Organizational Knowledge Creation*
Griselda Pollock's *Vision and Difference*
Amartya Sen's *Inequality Re-Examined*
Susan Sontag's *On Photography*
Yasser Tabbaa's *The Transformation of Islamic Art*
Ludwig von Mises's *Theory of Money and Credit*

The Macat Library By Discipline

Macat Disciplines

Access the greatest ideas and thinkers across entire disciplines, including

Postcolonial Studies

Roland Barthes's *Mythologies*
Frantz Fanon's *Black Skin, White Masks*
Homi K. Bhabha's *The Location of Culture*
Gustavo Gutiérrez's *A Theology of Liberation*
Edward Said's *Orientalism*
Gayatri Chakravorty Spivak's *Can the Subaltern Speak?*

Macat analyses are available from all good bookshops and libraries.

Access hundreds of analyses through one, multimedia tool.

Macat Disciplines

Access the greatest ideas and thinkers across entire disciplines, including

AFRICANA STUDIES

Chinua Achebe's *An Image of Africa: Racism in Conrad's Heart of Darkness*

W. E. B. Du Bois's *The Souls of Black Folk*

Zora Neale Hurston's *Characteristics of Negro Expression*

Martin Luther King Jr.'s *Why We Can't Wait*

Toni Morrison's *Playing in the Dark: Whiteness in the American Literary Imagination*

Macat analyses are available from all good bookshops and libraries.

Access hundreds of analyses through one, multimedia tool.

Macat Disciplines

Access the greatest ideas and thinkers across entire disciplines, including

FEMINISM, GENDER AND QUEER STUDIES

Simone De Beauvoir's
The Second Sex

Michel Foucault's
History of Sexuality

Betty Friedan's
The Feminine Mystique

Saba Mahmood's
*The Politics of Piety:
The Islamic Revival and
the Feminist Subject*

Joan Wallach Scott's
*Gender and the
Politics of History*

Mary Wollstonecraft's
*A Vindication of the
Rights of Woman*

Virginia Woolf's
A Room of One's Own

Judith Butler's
Gender Trouble

  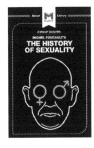 

Macat analyses are available from all good bookshops and libraries.

Access hundreds of analyses through one, multimedia tool.

Macat Disciplines

Access the greatest ideas and thinkers across entire disciplines, including

CRIMINOLOGY

Michelle Alexander's
The New Jim Crow: Mass Incarceration in the Age of Colorblindness

Michael R. Gottfredson & Travis Hirschi's
A General Theory of Crime

Elizabeth Loftus's
Eyewitness Testimony

Richard Herrnstein & Charles A. Murray's
The Bell Curve: Intelligence and Class Structure in American Life

Jay Macleod's
Ain't No Makin' It: Aspirations and Attainment in a Low-Income Neighborhood

Philip Zimbardo's
The Lucifer Effect

Macat analyses are available from all good bookshops and libraries.

Access hundreds of analyses through one, multimedia tool.

Macat Disciplines

Access the greatest ideas and thinkers across entire disciplines, including

INEQUALITY

Ha-Joon Chang's, *Kicking Away the Ladder*

David Graeber's, *Debt: The First 5000 Years*

Robert E. Lucas's, *Why Doesn't Capital Flow from Rich To Poor Countries?*

Thomas Piketty's, *Capital in the Twenty-First Century*

Amartya Sen's, *Inequality Re-Examined*

Mahbub Ul Haq's, *Reflections on Human Development*

  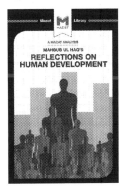

Macat analyses are available from all good bookshops and libraries.

Access hundreds of analyses through one, multimedia tool.

Join free for one month **library.macat.com**

Macat Disciplines

Access the greatest ideas and thinkers across entire disciplines, including

GLOBALIZATION

Arjun Appadurai's, *Modernity at Large: Cultural Dimensions of Globalisation*

James Ferguson's, *The Anti-Politics Machine*

Geert Hofstede's, *Culture's Consequences*

Amartya Sen's, *Development as Freedom*

Macat analyses are available from all good bookshops and libraries.

Access hundreds of analyses through one, multimedia tool.

Macat Disciplines

Access the greatest ideas and thinkers across entire disciplines, including

THE FUTURE OF DEMOCRACY

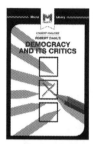

Robert A. Dahl's, *Democracy and Its Critics*
Robert A. Dahl's, *Who Governs?*
Alexis De Toqueville's, *Democracy in America*
Niccolò Machiavelli's, *The Prince*
John Stuart Mill's, *On Liberty*
Robert D. Putnam's, *Bowling Alone*
Jean-Jacques Rousseau's, *The Social Contract*
Henry David Thoreau's, *Civil Disobedience*

Macat Disciplines

*Access the greatest ideas and thinkers
across entire disciplines, including*

TOTALITARIANISM

Sheila Fitzpatrick's, *Everyday Stalinism*
Ian Kershaw's, *The "Hitler Myth"*
Timothy Snyder's, *Bloodlands*